Lightweight Touring

Cycling Across America with Just 12 Pounds of Gear, I Rode This Adventure and You Can Too!

Shawn A. Wakefield

Copyright © 2015 Shawn A. Wakefield and WakefieldSoft LLC.

All rights reserved. Edition 1.0.

www.LightweightBicycleTouring.com

ISBN: 1518692893

ISBN-13: 978-1518692895

DEDICATION

This book is dedicated to my lovely wife, who put up with me being on the road for two months during my cross country bicycle adventure. I would also like to acknowledge my children, parents, and friends for cheering me on from Oklahoma. Thanks to Bob Reynolds for initially having a crazy idea. Thanks to Ron Bull for shuttling us to the coast, selling a car, and tagging along for a few days. Also, thanks to Susan Hamilton who reviewed and helped edit the first manuscript. Finally, thanks be to God for life itself.

CONTENTS

INTRODUCTION 1

PRE-TRIP THOUGHTS 2
   The Idea 2
   What Ever Shall We Wear? 3
   When Shall We Go? 7
   Technology Anyone? 9
   To Train or Not to Train? 10
   Family Matters 11
   How Do You Start This Thing? 12

PREPARATIONS 15
   The Shake Down Ride 15
   The Week Before 16
   Our Training Summary 18

POST TRIP INFORMATION 20
   Gear Information and Details 20
   Water Topics 46
   Clothes Washing 47
   Cleaning Chains 48
   Fixing Flats 49
   Directions and Distances 51
   Riding the Shoulder 52
   Route Planning or Changing 54

OUR JOURNEY 57
   Georgia 59
   Florida 70
   Alabama 81
   Mississippi 85
   Louisiana 93
   Texas 121
   New Mexico 161
   Arizona 189
   California 215

INTRODUCTION

This book is written as an encouragement and help to anyone considering a long distance bike ride. I have encountered far too many riders carrying heavy loads; and these heavy loads can make a ride much more difficult and increase the chance of failure.

It is entirely possible to leave those 50, 60, or 80 pound loads behind and have a more enjoyable bicycle tour by travelling light. This book offers practical suggestions and advice for lightweight bicycle touring. I can honestly say that it is possible to reduce your gear weight to around 12 pounds, because I have done that, and then ridden across the country successfully.

Major sections of this book include my thoughts and experiences as a friend and I planned a coast to coast ride. The pre-trip thoughts will be helpful to others as they plan a cycling trip. Information compiled after our successful ride offers great details about our gear and all items selected and carried. Advice is also provided about practical aspects of the ride, and many of those topics were prompted by questions from others following our online journal.

Finally, my trip journal, with daily entries, is included as the last portion of this book. Readers can see exactly what the daily experience of a long distance ride might entail.

Whatever your dreams, I encourage you to start riding them. Whether it be 2600 miles on highways from coast to coast or 200 miles on a bike and pedestrian rails to trails project, bicycle touring can be enjoyed by nearly anyone.

Happy trails...

Shawn Wakefield

Shawn Wakefield

PRE-TRIP THOUGHTS

The Idea

What possesses a person to conceive of the idea to ride across the United States on a bicycle? The concept of weeks of riding, day after day, to cover several thousand miles would surely seem to be on the verge of insanity for most any reasonable person. It is not that it has never been done, for it has. It is not that it is impossible, for it is not. It is not that it is fraught with serious danger or peril, for it usually is not. But, perhaps, it was the idea that I had not yet done it. Perhaps it was that it seemed somewhat impossible for me, at least initially. Certainly, it seemed to be a method of seeing a wide swath of God's glorious creation at a relaxed speed.

In my case, I had planned a cross country ride, unsupported, with a lifelong friend. Let's call him Bob, for that is his name. Quite honestly, I cannot be sure who proposed the idea first. For you see, I have known Bob for several decades, and we have ridden hundreds of miles together over the course of those years. We no longer live close to each other, but for some friends, that distance is not a hindrance to the friendship. So it is the case with my friend Bob. As Bob tells the story, he has dreamed of riding his bicycle across the country since he was in his teens, and he is now in his sixties. From my perspective, I recall talking with Bob about the challenge of such an endeavor when I was in my teens, and I am now in my forties. Time, circumstance, responsibilities, and life had simply prevented such an attempt, until recently.

Bob and I began discussing this possibility well over a year before our ride. And as I typed these words, we were still two months away from starting our adventure, but it was many months ago that Bob reminded me of his lifelong dream. I told Bob that if I could manage to retire early, then I would join him and we could attempt this crazy idea together. Well, early retirement had come (that could be the topic of another book), and so plans were made. My goal for this writing is to share our planning of the adventure, and then details of the adventure itself. In so doing, I also want to encourage others by explaining that gear weight, often well over fifty pounds, need not be so heavy or such an obstacle. So, there we were, in late December before our spring ride, readying ourselves mentally and physically for an endurance test of approximately two months. I was very excited about this adventure, and it was an excellent trip to celebrate my recent retirement.

I have been a bicyclist off and on for 30 years. Bob and I rode many miles together while I was in high school and college. We have even ridden a handful of century, or 100 mile, rides. My riding recently has been more infrequent, but the love of cycling has remained. It may be the thought of being able to propel yourself so easily across the pavement at many times the speed of walking that has always seemed so efficient to me. Riding a basic machine, weighing only a few dozen pounds, which can convert a smooth pedaling motion into a significant speed for a human being is refreshing. This process produces no smog, no pollution, and has only a few moving parts to replace. The whole concept is wonderful, even idealistic. With such a machine, we planned to undertake a grand adventure.

What Ever Shall We Wear?

We both already had bicycles. I have owned old ten speeds, road bikes, and even an electric bike. I am sure that it has been the same with Bob, but for a continuous ride of more than 2500 miles, it seemed logical to upgrade our equipment in order to improve the odds of a successful ride. Now, a new bike purchase for such a ride as this could allow for a great range of expenditures. Certainly, many have ridden this distance with bicycles that were decades old. On the other end of the spectrum, it is possible to easily spend several thousand dollars for a custom made bicycle. We chose the middle ground, each purchasing a quality steel frame touring bike. The touring bike is similar to a road bike, but with some enhancements to assist in a long distance ride. Primarily the touring bike will include features such as a longer wheelbase, higher number of spokes, and a larger range of gears. The primary advantage of more gears, especially lower gears, is that it allows for easier climbs on steeper hills. In my lowest gear, climbing a large hill, I could still be pedaling but rolling as slow as 3 mph.

We actually each bought identical model bikes, of the appropriate frame size for each of us. Since we both planned to invest in a touring bike, we decided that having identical bicycles with common parts would allow us to carry a smaller set of tools, spare tubes, and so forth. This would reduce the number and weight of bike related supplies and repair items that would need to be carried. This falls in line with my personal ideals of efficiency and travelling light. I am also a lightweight backpacker, and in that pursuit I always strive to travel light and only carry items that have multiple uses. I do realize that having identical equipment is not possible for many riders that ride such a distance with others, but for our attempt it was practical. I do not mention brand names intentionally, and I will try to avoid that action throughout this writing. Brand names change, prices change, and even quality comparisons between brands can change over the years. If you are interested in a long distance touring ride, then please do your own research to determine what might work best for your goals. I will reveal that our bicycles were in the $1500 price range.

Regarding gear, I will do my best to describe what we carried, but our gear list may not work ideally for others. As I mentioned, I love lightweight backpacking. Those lightweight concepts were applied to how we intended to travel. We had read many journals of others that have ridden across the country, and we had seen photos of bicycles with four saddle bags, or panniers. We had also noticed that many riders pull small trailers loaded with gear, many of those with over one hundred pounds of gear on that trailer! For us, that just seemed to be an enormous amount of weight to have to propel up and down mountains, across deserts, and through the rain. Alternately, there are many who choose to ride each day, but stay in hotels every night and eat all of their meals in a restaurant. This was not our desire. As with backpacking, the idea of carrying everything we needed to survive, at least for a few days, evoked frontiersmen type feelings. The feeling of being self-sufficient and conquering obstacles by ourselves was thrilling.

As I describe gear, I will begin with the bags in which it will all be carried. There are numerous brands and styles of panniers. Front, rear, waterproof, heavy, light, large, and small are just a few of the styles. Many of the models available weigh five pounds or more. This just seemed to be much more weight than was necessary for an empty bag. We chose a dry bag style pannier that weighed about one pound for the pair. The volume was not quite as large as others, but this would actually force us to carry fewer items and make very careful choices about our equipment. In addition, we opted to only use rear panniers. Front panniers were not used, but we knew that we might use a handlebar bag or trunk (rear rack) bag. We simply did not want to carry more weight, and so front panniers were not taken. All of our gear would have to fit in the rear bags. At the early stage in our planning, we were hoping to carry 20 pounds, or less, of gear each. We clearly achieved that goal.

The gear selection process was a complex one. Whether or not riders plan to sleep in a tent and cook some of their own meals will have a large impact on what items should be carried. We planned to sleep in a tent most nights, and only use a hotel once a week or so. For shelter, we planned to carry a lightweight tent, which was really more like a tarp with a floor and some netting. The weight for this shelter, ground sheet, and stakes should be about 2.5 pounds or less, although even lighter solutions are available. We wanted the ability to cook our own meals, even if we did eat in many cafes or restaurants for convenience during the day. This decision meant that we needed to carry some type of cook kit. We planned to use a lightweight alcohol stove and aluminum pot. This would allow us to boil water and make noodles, coffee, oatmeal, and other hot meals. As with backpacking, I usually select meals that only require boiling water. The hot water can then be added to noodles or other foods in a Ziploc quart freezer bag. This eliminates the need for cleaning cooking pans, and it also keeps them cleaner and eliminates any food smells that might attract wildlife.

Along with shelter, tent camping also requires a sleeping bag and optional ground pad. Traditional sleeping bags can certainly be used, but I prefer a down quilt. This backpacking quilt is essentially the top half of a sleeping bag. Since insulation under the body is compressed, down on the bottom offers little insulation value. A backpacking quilt has a foot box to slip your feet into, and then it covers the top of the body and tucks under your sides or shoulders. This down quilt option provides comfort in temperatures down to freezing, and it only weighs approximately one pound. It is also possible to find lightweight traditional sleeping bags with down insulation that weigh between one and two pounds. Since the quilt does not have a bottom, it is helpful to sleep on a thin foam pad or light inflatable pad. I usually select a closed cell foam pad that is about 1/4 inch thick, and then put a light inflatable pad on top of that. This setup keeps my total pad weight under one pound, but provides some level of comfort and insulation from the cold or hard ground. The foam pad can also be omitted, and a person could carry only the inflatable pad, or vice versa.

In contrast to those who stay in hotels every night, also known as credit card touring, we had planned haul a tent and sleeping gear. Carrying these carefully chosen, lightweight items would enable us to stop riding and camp at any point. For around five pounds of camping gear weight, we would have the option of ending our day at an optimal time, regardless of our location. We would not be forced to push into the night to reach a town, and we could camp nearly anywhere along the road. This option would provide great freedom in route planning and daily mileages. In addition, we hoped to find many amazing and peaceful campsites. We would have the privilege of combining biking and camping, which was ideal for us. We would also be able to keep our total tour costs more reasonable. Stealth camping along our route would be free, but even if we chose to tent camp in a state park or RV park, the nightly costs are usually very low. If we could find state parks or RV parks at convenient locations, those often would provide shower facilities as well. We had also considered checking into WarmShowers.org as an option, but that was still something that we were thinking about early in the planning process. Our actual ride did not end up as we had planned, and more about that will be explained later.

Another major gear category is clothing. We were planning to go minimal here as well. Of course, we would need biking clothes, but at an early stage we were planning for only two sets of socks, shorts, and jerseys. We had planned to carry leggings and sleeves to provide for full coverage on cold mornings. Town clothes would be used to slip on at town stops, primarily a pair of convertible hiking pants and a long sleeve shirt. These items could also double as extra layers for cold times in camp, and we could even sleep in the extra layers on cold nights. The only additional items of clothing on our list were a rain jacket, knit stocking cap, full finger gloves, and a lightweight down vest. As it turned out, we actually only carried one set of biking clothes, and this worked out just fine.

Bike specific gear would be shared. We planned to carry two spare tubes and a spare folding tire, along with a patch kit. We expected this to be sufficient, since towns would allow us to replace used tubes. We would be each carrying a pump. Since this item was critical to keep tires properly inflated or fix flats, we decided that we would duplicate this one item. Other bike items included a tool kit that could adjust or tighten all sizes of screws and bolts on our bikes. We would also carry a spare chain link and chain tool, although most riders seems to rarely have any chain issues. The touring bikes included spare spokes, and we would make sure that our brake pads had plenty of life left on them.

Safety was a major concern, and several gear items were related to safety. We did not intend to ride after dark, but sometimes that might not be avoidable. We both had equipped our touring bikes with head lights and tail lights. The tail lights, as with most, had a flashing mode, and we thought we might use the flashing mode on our tail lights even during the day, at least for the rider in back. We wanted to be as visible as possible to traffic approaching from the rear. Our light choices happened to be rechargeable by USB, which was a convenient option. Our phone charging cord would also be able to charge our lights. Although we had not finalized our safety gear early in our planning process, we did consider wearing neon safety green vests over our clothing if we had to wear jackets or other clothing that was not brightly colored. We ended up not wearing the vests. We had also tried to locate reflective safety triangles to attach to the back of our rear racks. Finally, one of us did use a small flag pole attached to the rear rack. This improved visibility, may have been a conversation starter in towns, and was fashioned from one of the tent poles, thus being a dual purpose item. I ordered three flags (American, Oklahoma, and Christian flags), all 4 inches by 6 inches in size. I attached those to a tube of black fabric to attach the pole.

Not surprisingly, some of the gear choices changed based on our trip experience. Please see the post trip section for detailed gear lists and weights.

When Shall We Go?

There are numerous bicycling routes across the United States, although many are not well marked or identified. Many are well established, if not by the states, then by the Adventure Cycling Association. For our purposes, a southern route seemed to be the best fit. I live in Oklahoma, and my friend Bob lives in Arizona. A southerly route would take us close to, if not through, these two states. The southern tier route, established by the Adventure Cycling Association stays very close to the southern border of the United States, beginning in Florida and ending in San Diego, California. We planned a modified version of this route. We intended to start at Jekyll Island, along the coast in southern Georgia. We would be on portions of the official southern tier route along the Gulf Coast, and then again in Arizona and California. We planned to angle north into Oklahoma during the middle of our route. With this approximate route identified, the When question could be more easily answered based on seasonal temperatures. Following my retirement in December, the soonest that we could attempt a ride was the first half of 2015. With the route being in the south portion of the United States, the best time of year to ride was early spring or early fall. With all of those variables, many being fixed, we had scheduled our tour to occur in March and April.

A few comments could be made on route selection at this point. You can certainly choose a route based on what area of the country you would like to cross. There are northern routes, diagonal routes, north to south routes, and so on. Even if you choose an established route, you may want to make changes based on the latest state maps. Some states publish bike maps showing which highways are bike friendly, but at this point in time, that is not the norm. One amazing tool that we used to help select certain segments was Google Street View. Using this method, we could spot check nearly any road in the country to see if it had shoulders, was four lane, etc. With the street view, we could view the road as if we were standing on it and looking in either direction. We also made slight modifications based on some online tour journals. We found one segment near Globe, Arizona that was described as harrowing by many riders. We selected an alternate route in this area. Finally, although we had a good guess of our tour route, we did not follow it perfectly. We expected that changes, reroutes, and detours would be part of the journey, and they were. These changes helped to keep the experience fresh and challenging. On one hand, safety urged us to try to select safe roads. On the other hand, we hoped that we had not planned it too carefully in order to preserve much of the mystery and excitement of this personal adventure.

With a route in place, and the time of the year selected, the next question, although perhaps not obvious to all, was "What direction shall we ride?" Much debate regarding this question can be found in books and online journals. The prevailing thought seemed to be that riding west to east will allow the rider to take advantage of more tailwinds. This was certainly worthy of some consideration, but on closer reading and research, winds are simply not always reliably blowing from west to east. First, any cross country ride will have many angles and zig zags, causing the rider to have to ride directions other than straight east or west. Winds at ground level are often not the same as winds aloft, and may not follow the Jetstream. It seemed from a more careful reading that cross winds from the south are as likely as tailwinds from the west, thus eliminating some advantage of riding west to east.

For our trip, we traversed a thought process similar to what follows. Since mountains are not close to the east coast, but mountains are close to the west coast - just outside of San Diego; a ride starting in the west would immediately put a rider into a long climb early in the tour. Starting from the east, initial riding days would be relatively flat, and longer mountain climbs would generally be delayed until the later weeks of the trip, and presumably when we would be more conditioned. This would be one vote for an east to west route. Also, descending from the mountains near the west coast would allow the rider to see the Pacific Ocean for some time before reaching it, thus building a degree of anticipation for the completion of the tour. Basic geography would prevent this from being the case if finishing in the east at the Atlantic Ocean. This would be an additional vote for an east to west route. For some riders, the location of home might be closer to one coast or the other, but for myself in Oklahoma, this was not really an advantage one way or the other. Finally, although more philosophical than practical, this great country was settled by pioneers from east to west. We thought that it would be great to ride east to west in the same direction as those early settlers. I realize that Native Americans were already here, and I am of Cherokee ancestry myself, so I will simply choose to put any debate on those type of matters aside for the time being. In total, we felt that there were several valid reasons, for us anyway, for riding from east to west, and that those would outweigh the unreliable hope of prevailing westerly winds.

After our trip was finished, I sat down and analyzed the winds and riding direction for each day of our journey. For our trip, of the days with any significant wind, we experienced cross winds (generally from the north or south) about 40% of the time. We experienced tail winds (generally from the east) about 30% of the time, and we experienced head winds (generally from west) about 30% of the time. In our case, the winds did not show any advantage in riding from west to east. It is possible that this would be different in other years or times of the year, but we were extremely happy with our choice of direction.

With our riding direction established, I would like to elaborate more on our dates. This timing would normally, as much as weather can be considered normal, allow us to start riding after most of the winter weather has retreated from the southeast. We knew that we might have occasional cold nights, but most of the daytime temperatures were moderate. With our down sleeping equipment, and wearing all of our clothing, an occasional night into the 20s would still be tolerable. Late March and into April are fine times to ride, with numerous beautiful days. This time frame was that of our journey up into Oklahoma and west across Texas and New Mexico. We travelled through the desert areas of Arizona in mid to late April, which allowed us to beat the extreme desert heat. The time period was also the soonest that we could realistically put together such a ride. This certainly spoke of the strong desire to embark on this challenge as soon as it was practically possible for each of us.

Technology Anyone?

In this day, it seems everyone is connected, myself included. Many of us cannot sit still for five minutes without picking up our phone to play games or check messages. With nationwide connectivity, we could have certainly been connected every minute on a cross country ride. However, for me, that stood in contradiction to the physical challenge and philosophy of crossing the country under my own power. Should other aspects of the ride be adjusted in order to prevent the dilution of the human challenge? While global positioning systems allow constant directions and turn by turn navigation, I chose not to use a GPS or even my phone as a navigation tool unless we were wildly off course. Bob had a biking GPS and we did consider it for complicated inner city wayfinding, but for the most part, I intended to carry some cut down paper state maps and keep technology to a minimum during the actual riding experience. This did, in some way, help to maintain the mystique and romance of such an east to west, coast to coast, ride.

Another reason to keep technology turned off is a more practical one - power. A GPS, or even a phone running a GPS app, will only be able to run on average one day on a full charge. In planning to camp along the route most nights, we had eliminated typical sources of power to recharge devices. We did intend to carry phones to communicate with family and friends, but they were turned off much of the day. This preserved battery life, and we had hoped that it would allow our phones to last three or four days on a single charge with limited use. We would not be able to use the phone while riding (remember, don't text and drive), so the device might as well be turned off to save power.

The only other electronic device that I had intended to carry was a small tablet. These sizes are more portable, lighter, smaller, and have longer battery life than larger tablets. You might wonder why a tablet would be carried if we had a phone with us. In many respects, the tablet was not at all necessary. However, the tablet did function as an eBook reader, which we thought might come in handy when we had some free time. Also, when we were in towns with Wi-Fi, perhaps at a cafe or restaurant, this device allowed more convenient web browsing and journal updating. Also, with only a few hours use each day, the tablet lasted for several days between charges. Finally, writing this manuscript was considerably more convenient because I was able to type daily entries each evening using a small Bluetooth keyboard and a tablet.

Now, the issue with carrying a couple of devices was charging them. If we had only stayed at a hotel once a week, then we could only fully charge once a week. In our case, we chose a USB battery pack (10,400 mAh capacity) to allow one or two charges of each device during the week from the portable battery pack. With this lightweight pack, we only needed one night with electricity every 7 or 8 days. In addition to being able to charge our tablet and phone, this charging pack would also charge our headlights and tail lights as needed. Rather than needing to carry disposable batteries, both lights had built in battery packs that allowed them to be recharged via a USB cable. We were also able to carry only one or two cables and charge any device. This might seem like a significant number of devices, and we thought we might opt to send a few items back once the ride began, but the setup worked well for us.

To Train or Not to Train?

I am certain, with as many cross country tours that happen each year, numerous riders attempt such a feat with all manner of training backgrounds. There likely are riders who have ridden every day for some time before they start a cross country ride. I would venture to say that there just as many riders who ride very little before a tour. It is simply a matter of probability and human nature that would dictate that all points along the training spectrum be represented. Similarly, it is the same with Appalachian Trail through hikers, those that attempt the entire trail in one season. This long distance trail fascinates me, and I have read many accounts of those attempting to conquer the entire length of it. I have only spent a week on the trail, putting about 80 miles behind me, but so many others have done much more with less training. Many hikers prepare for many months while others start a hike without any training whatsoever.

So it is bound to be similar on cross country bicycle rides. Bob had ridden most days of the week over the last year or more before our trip, but I had only managed a weekly ride, more or less, over the last six months before the first of the year. I intended to ramp up my training regimen over the 6 or 8 weeks before the ride, trying to ride most every day of the week and then one longer ride once a week. Just as many hikers start the Appalachian Trail and allow the first few weeks of the hike to be their training, we thought that we might do a similar thing. We did have some advantages over those new to biking. First, we had ridden for many years, granted some of those years did not see many miles, but we hoped to be able to keep daily mileages lower for the first week or so. Second, I was in relatively good shape and appropriate weight for my height. A pound of flesh might as well be a pound of unused gear for such an adventure as this. Finally, I planned to use my lightweight backpacking experience to my advantage. Our gear selection and quantity would be lighter than most, and I was used to camping and cooking away from civilization. None of these, even in aggregate, could guarantee success, but we hoped that the odds would be in our favor. The low gear weight did turn out to be a major advantage.

Although Bob and I live in different states, we planned to get to together about 10 days before the start of our ride to finalize equipment, tweak our route, and train together. We planned to ride daily, although it was not a typical touring day's distance. It was more difficult to get motivated to ride 40 or 50 miles alone, without moving from one place to the next, as we would on a tour. However, we did agree that a gear shakedown would be helpful. To this end, we planned and executed an overnight training trip before our tour. We rode over 30 miles to a state park campground, spent the night and cooked our meals, and then returned the next day. This did provide an opportunity to verify that all of our gear was correct, adequate, and not containing too many luxuries.

Family Matters

I would like to include some narrative regarding being away from one's family. In my case, I am married to a wonderful Christian woman and had been for more than 23 years at the start of our ride. We also have three children. For this trip, she was not following behind in a vehicle, primarily due to two of our children still living at home. Thankfully, she was supportive of my adventure with Bob. I understand that not all spouses may be so inclined. In other instances, both spouses may share the love of biking and take a trip together. Jana was not someone who likes to bicycle long distances, and that was perfectly fine. At some future point, she might be able to follow in a support vehicle, or we might take a shorter ride as an entire family. As it turned out, Jana did ride over 200 miles on the Katy Trail with me while this manuscript was still being edited and reworked. Way to go!

To some extent, not wanting to be away from my family for too long did influence our route and timing. Approximately two weeks into the ride, spring break would allow my family to drive east and meet us for a day or two. About half way through the ride, we planned to ride through southern Oklahoma and be able to spend a few nights at my home. Then, about two weeks west of the midpoint, I had hoped that at least my wife, and perhaps the family, would drive out to see us for a day or so. Finally, my friend Bob lives in Phoenix, and we planned to ride through Phoenix to be able to spend a couple of nights at his place.

Although being away from my family was not ideal, we thought we had worked it out in this case to be no more than two weeks apart at a time. It turned out to not be that frequent in the second half of our trip. Thankfully, current technology did allow us to talk, text, and video chat at many points along the way. I also posted journal entries of our mileages and progress to allow family and friends to see some photos and follow our route from home.

How Do You Start This Thing?

For many, the logistical challenge of getting yourself and your equipment to the starting point is significant. For myself, living in the Midwest, I am not close to either coast, so two issues had to be resolved - getting to the start, and returning from the finish.

There are several options for arriving at the starting point for a tour. Usually, airports are not close to the beach, so even flying leaves a final leg that must be travelled by car. Certainly bicycles can be boxed and shipped. This is easier by ground than air, but we wanted to avoid these options. Call me paranoid, but I had this nightmare where I shipped my bike to the east coast, arrived by plane, and found my bike damaged beyond repair. Since there were two of us, driving would not be much more costly than flying. Once at the coast, we simply had to find someone to get the car back home. We could have picked up someone that flew out to the east coast to drive back, or we could have driven out with friends and family, and they could have driven the car back home.

Our solution seemed like it would work out quite well. My wife's parents wanted to see Savannah, Georgia. Jekyll Island was not too far from Savannah. We planned to all drive out, bikes included, and then they could sightsee, visit Savannah, and take their time returning home with the car. We could drive to the east coast in two days, so we would need a few hotel nights, but we could take our time and set our own schedule. Having a vehicle of our own would make it much easier to get to the coast to dip our back wheels ceremoniously in the Atlantic surf.

At the other edge of the continent, in San Diego, the situation was different but manageable. From the planned ending point, the Amtrak Station was about seven miles away. This is an inconsequential distance after such a long bicycle ride. We planned to spend the night at a hotel after completed our tour, ride our bikes to the train station, and box them up to go with us back to Dallas. Amtrak is more bike friendly than any airline, and any mechanical damage would not be a serious issue during our return trip. The cost to ship a bike was minimal, and it could be checked on the same train that we rode. The fares by rail were reasonable, and Dallas was only two hours from my home, allowing any friend or family member to come and retrieve us.

Those were the plans, but reality did not exactly match our plans.

Soon after making what seemed to be excellent plans, things soon changed. For certain reasons, we did not have anyone available to drive out with us or fly out and drive the car back. My family also ended up buying a newer, used car just a few weeks before the trip was supposed to start. I found myself needing to sell our Chevy Malibu before the trip, if possible. My mother-in-law suggested that we just drive the old car to the east coast and sell it before starting the ride. Now, mothers-in-law can sometimes make less than welcome suggestions to many sons-in-law, and at first, I thought that this idea could well have been one of them!

So, we looked at other ways of getting to the east coast. We wanted to avoid shipping the bikes if at all possible. The chance of arriving at the starting point, and then opening our bikes up from the shipping cartons and finding major damage was just too risky. We considered the bus, but the primary bus line we looked into did not allow bikes as checked baggage. Amtrak was known as a bike friendly option, so we researched taking the train.

Amtrak presented several issues from Oklahoma. First, we would need to drive to Dallas in order to avoid being on four different train routes. Second, since we would be on three different train routes, we would need to pull our bikes from the train and spend nights in both San Antonio and New Orleans. Finally, it would be a three day journey by train just to get to Atlanta, and we would still need to find a way to the coast. The cost would be about $500 or more for the both of us, which is considerably higher than the $100 or so in fuel to drive to Georgia.

As we considered our options, it seemed that Jana's mother's idea to drive the car east and sell it might be worth some consideration. (Did I really just type that last sentence?)

To me, the primary issue of selling the car after we drove it out was one of practicality. We did not have much time to sell it personally, and used car dealers usually only want to give the trade in value. Well, I have a good friend from high school, Ron, who lives near Knoxville, Tennessee. I knew him well enough to think that he might just be interested in a crazy idea like this. I called Ron and pitched my wild idea. We brainstormed a bit, and after some discussion concocted the following plan. We would drive the Malibu to Knoxville with our bicycles. Ron had a trusted friend, Steve, at his church. Steve was not a dealer, but buys and sells vehicles online, and he agreed to sell the Malibu for me. Ron would transport the two of us, and the bikes, from Knoxville to Jekyll Island. Ron also was interested in following us for a couple of days, just in case we had any issues at the start of our trip. Ron would then return to Knoxville after we had ridden about half way across Georgia.

It could very well be the most unorthodox method of arriving at the coast to start a bicycle tour, but it seemed to be all worked out. We drove the car east, the car was sold, and we bicycled west without anyone having to drive a vehicle back to Oklahoma. As a bonus, our bicycles travelled with us, in our care, and never left our sight. Unorthodox, yes, but it turned out to be a great idea.

PREPARATIONS

The Shake Down Ride

We wanted to test all of our gear and see how things worked before we were all the way at the Atlantic Ocean. About 10 days before our trip, we loaded all of our gear on the bikes and rode 33 miles from Tishomingo to Sulphur, Oklahoma. We camped at the Chickasaw National Recreation Area. Bob's Senior Pass allowed us to camp for only $7.00 at a tent site with no utilities. Not bad.

The ride over all was very good, with a slight tail wind. We rode the 33 miles in less than 3 hours with an average speed of just over 12 miles per hour. Our top speed during the ride was 38 miles per hour! This was downhill, of course. One memorable scene on the trip was a couple of horses running out in the pasture as we rode by. We noted that it would be important to make note of the "neat things" that we experienced during our journey.

We set up the tent, laid out our bedding, and then boiled water on the alcohol stove for dinner. We made dehydrated spaghetti and also ramen noodles. The low temperature was only supposed to be 40 degrees, so we expected a nice night. With not much to do, we were in the tent by 7pm, staying warm and taking it easy.

The night was cold and breezy in the tent, with a low of about 42 degrees. When we woke up the next morning, the sky was overcast, and the winds were about 10 to 15 mph and in a direction to provide a head wind. We boiled water for oatmeal, ate some trail mix, and were on the road by 10am, somewhat later than planned, but we were hoping it would warm up. This was not to be as the temperatures ranged from 42 to 46 degrees all the way back home, and with that head wind, the wind chill was in the mid-30s. This was definitely a cold riding day. We stopped at Mill Creek for a couple of bacon cheeseburgers, hot coffee, and other snacks. This was a welcome stop for us, and it provided time to warm up. With more fuel for our engine, we headed south again, making better progress and staying warmer than before. We made a few more break stops, and arrived back in Tishomingo in the early afternoon. We averaged 9.1 mph back over those 33 miles. This was not a bad speed, considering the cold temperatures and head wind.

It was also quite humorous on a couple of occasions. At Mill Creek, Bob had stopped, but was too tired to pull his leg up and over his bike without me holding it steady. Two cafe patrons asked him if he was alright as they were leaving. And then, at another stop at a convenience store in Ravia, Bob went out the door first, looking quite fatigued. Before I left, the clerk asked me if he was OK. She had actually offered him a chair to rest in twice! I told her that "he has no balance, and can hardly walk, but once he gets back on his bike he will be fine." I expected that our tour would be one funny day after another with Bob as my companion.

Several good things came out of this practice trip. We planned to carry a few more matches than normal, since the wind made the stove hard to light. Our clothes were adequate, but we hoped to not have to ride in any weather below 45 degrees, if possible. We had some additional thoughts and ideas about food and packing that would be helpful as well. More details on this will be included later.

Our campsite for the shake down ride. That cuben fiber tent is less than one pound for the tent, stakes, and pole!

The Week Before

The weather in Oklahoma was terrible the week before we departed. We did make the most of our time in planning and preparing. It was difficult to ride in the weather - freezing rain, sleet, snow, and some days not above freezing.

The last day or so we had worked very hard on route planning. Our plan was to generally follow the southern tier of the Adventure Cycling Association with a diversion up to Tishomingo, Oklahoma. Bob had purchased a Garmin cycling GPS, which included online software to do route planning. We could have used Google Maps, I am sure, but the Garmin software proved to work quite well.

By starting at Jekyll Island, we decided to plan our own route through Georgia, and we would not meet up with the southern tier until Chattahoochee, Florida. We would generally follow the southern tier through the rest of Florida, Alabama, Mississippi, and Louisiana to New Roads, Louisiana. From New Roads, we planned to angle northwest through Louisiana, the corner of Texas, and then into Oklahoma. Once we left Tishomingo, Oklahoma, we planned to angle down into Texas, heading west into New Mexico and across Arizona. We would be north of the southern tier route until Phoenix. At Phoenix, we would again follow the southern tier to San Diego.

By plotting the entire route and downloading it to the GPS, we had the ability to use that device for any tricky turns or in complicated cities along the route. Primarily, we planned to navigate using paper maps. We had highlighted and cut up state maps, copied and printed other maps, and would also carry the relevant southern tier maps. I had a handlebar bag, which had a clear map pocket for viewing paper maps while riding. This bag worked very well for me on the tour.

We soon had the planned route plotted and uploaded to the GPS. We also had a complete set of paper maps that we could follow. With these items, we felt confident that we had all of the tools necessary to navigate.

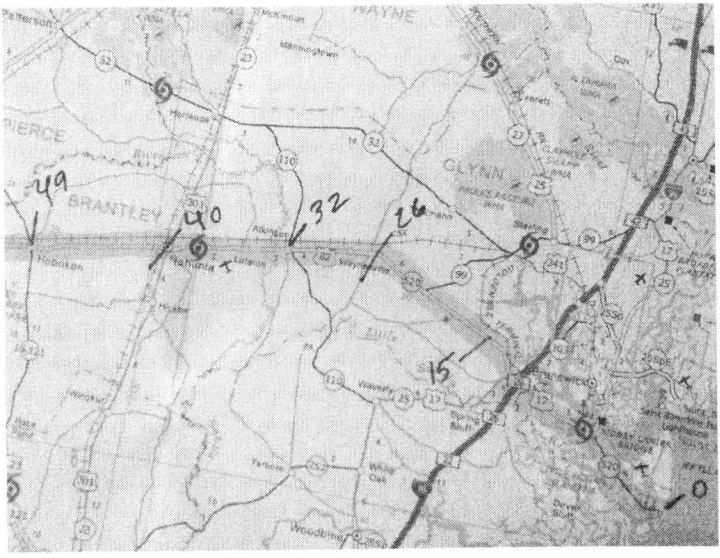

On each map that was a state highway map, I measured and marked mileages to make it easier to see what points of interest might be along the road.

Lightweight Bicycle Touring

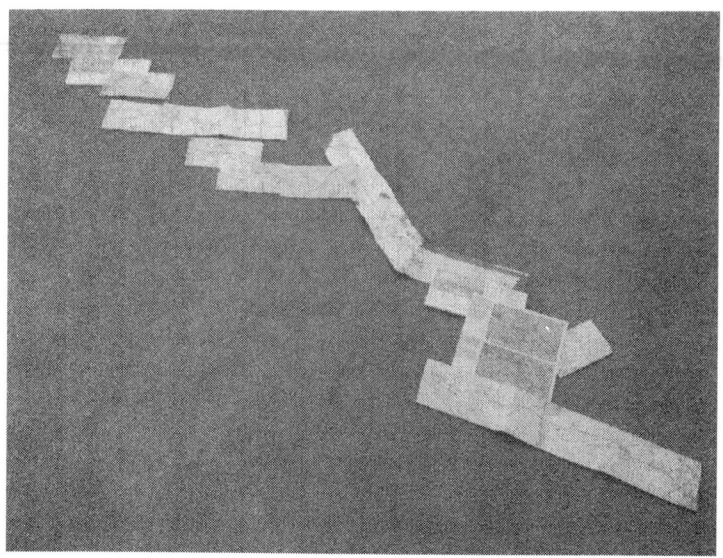

The entire route, strung out across numerous maps. The route changed, but this was a good best guess.

Our Training Summary

I am sure that all kinds of people have all kinds of training regimens. For myself, living in Oklahoma, training can be somewhat challenging, or at least cold, during the months of January and February. I had been riding to work off and on for the last six or nine months, but I had not been putting in big miles. I did some research about training and made a plan to start in early January with my training rides. The details are not so important, but I wanted to ride several days a week. I also wanted to increase my weekly mileage totals to be over 100 miles by the week before our trip.

Plans do not always work out, which was the case with my training rides. I knew it would not be possible to ride as much as we would be riding on the trip, but I was hoping for enough long rides that my legs would be strengthened. Our 66 mile shake down trip, with an overnight camping stay, was two weeks before our trip, not the week before. However, it was a great ride, nonetheless.

I was able to log about 500 miles of riding during January and February. My highest mileage week was about 100 miles. I am sure there would be many that would say that I had not trained nearly enough, but I felt very good during our actual tour. We knew that we could also adjust distances during the start of our trip to work ourselves up to higher daily mileages if necessary.

I guess that I took a similar approach to our bike ride that many take that hike the entire Appalachian Trail. It is possible to train very hard and be ready to go long distances from the first day. However, many hikers simply let the start of the journey be their training hikes. As they become stronger, then they are able to hike longer distances. For our trip, especially starting from the east coast with flat terrain, we would be able to pace ourselves and treat the first week as a training week of sorts.

POST TRIP INFORMATION

With our trip complete, I have compiled information and advice based on our two months of bicycle touring. If you are planning a tour, this section will be extremely helpful. I felt that it was important to place this information before our journal, in case some people would not want to read the entire trip journal. The major change from our plans was related to camping. We ended up staying in hotels and motels in order for Bob to get more rest, which was likely easier for me as well. I will still address the camping aspect in my discussion that follows, since I have camped many nights during lightweight backpacking trips.

Gear Information and Details

Some gear information has been mentioned previously, but this gear discussion will be based on our actual trip experience. First of all, we found that nearly every other tourer that we met was carrying much more gear than necessary. Many riders seemed to have 60 to 100 pounds of gear loaded on their bikes. We worked hard to travel light, and we even lightened our loads as we went. This made our ride much easier and more enjoyable.

The table below lists all gear that was initially carried. I will make note of those items that would only be needed if camping. Our total gear weight was **under 12 pounds per person**, with about 3.5 pounds of that being camping related and not necessary if a rider stayed only in hotels or motels.

GEAR WEIGHT GRAND TOTALS		Shawn	Bob
	Pounds	11.8	10.6

Bicycle Related Items	Wt (g)	Wt (oz)	
Bicycle: REI Novara Randonee Touring			
Fenders: Planet Bike Cascadia Hybrid			Total gear weight does not include bicycle weight, attached items, worn items, food, or water. These tend to be fixed for any given rider or trip.
Headlight: CatEye Volt 300 USB	114	4.0	
Tail Light: Cygolite Hotshot USB	46	1.6	
Pump: Topeak Road Morph G	206	7.3	
Computer: Planet Bike Protege 9	25	0.9	
Panniers: Arkel Dry-Lites	505	17.8	
Handle Bar Bag: Banjo Brothers Medium	495	17.5	
Water bottles, Qty 2, 28 oz, w/ duct tape	172	6.1	
Flag Stick Stand / Tent Pole / Flags	135	4.8	

Clothing	Shawn (g)	Shawn (oz)	Bob (g)	Bob (oz)
Shoes, MTB style, cleated (worn)				
Bike Shorts (worn)				
Bike Shirt, high visibility (worn)				
Bike Gloves, fingerless (worn)				
Socks, synthetic, ankle (worn)				
Helmet, high visibility, with mirror (worn)				
Long Sleeve Shirt, synthetic	154	5.4	163	5.7
Long Pants, hiking, convertible	285	10.1	299	10.5
Underwear, extra, for sleeping, quick dry	53	1.9	61	2.2
Rain Gear: Jacket	172	6.1	172	6.1
Rain Gear: Pants	70	2.5		
Alternate Footwear, light sandals	190	6.7		
Down Vest, ultralight, medium	106	3.7	196	6.9

Base Layer Top, black, silk	90	3.2		
Fleece Cap, beanie style	26	0.9		
Balaclava, head cover, for under helmet	32	1.1	33	1.2
Leggings, legs only	115	4.1	119	4.2
Sleeves, arms only	57	2.0	57	2.0
Warm Gloves, with fingers	97	3.4	104	3.7
Head Band, ear cover, quick dry	19	0.7		
Helmet Cover, windproof, neon	14	0.5		
Socks, synthetic, ankle, 2nd pair	31	1.1	27	1.0
Glasses, prescription, in case	83	2.9	70	2.5
Total Clothing		**56.2**		**45.9**

Miscellaneous	Shawn (g)	Shawn (oz)	Bob (g)	Bob (oz)
Bicycle Repair: tube, patches, tools, rags, oil, chain link, zip ties, bolts, pliers	421	14.9	470	16.6
Bike lock, cable and key	120	4.2		
Dog Repellent, Halt	67	2.4		
Knife, small, lightweight	18	0.6		
Whistle, orange, plastic	7	0.2		
Wallet (lightweight), Emergency info, Info cards	38	1.3	76	2.7
Maps, in plastic bag	81	2.9		
Paper and pencil, in bag	17	0.6		
Quick dry towel, REI	82	2.9	86	3.0
Hand Sanitizer, 2 oz	67	2.4		
Bug repel, 0.5 oz spray	22	0.8		
Photon Micro Light	7	0.2		
Small Rope, clothes line, tie down	18	0.6		
Total Miscellaneous		**34.0**		**22.3**

First Aid	Shawn (g)	Shawn (oz)	Bob (g)	Bob (oz)
First Aid Kit: Needle/thread, safety pin(2), antibiotic ointment, sting relief(2), alcohol pads(2), bandaids(8), throat lozenges(2), decongestant(10), antihistamine(2), Rolaids(6), Imodium(2), pepto(2), 2x3 pad(3), body glide	62	2.2	66	2.3
Nail trimmers	15	0.5		
Tweezers	8	0.3		
Earplugs (2)	1	0.0		
Total First Aid		**3.0**		**2.3**

Toiletries or Personal Hygiene	Shawn (g)	Shawn (oz)	Bob (g)	Bob (oz)
Vitamins / Meds / Ibuprofen in case	76	2.7	357	12.6
Soap, peppermint, 2 oz bottle	40	1.4		
Sunscreen, 1 oz tube	26	0.9		
Toilet Paper	26	0.9	14	0.5
Toothpaste, small	14	0.5		
Floss	14	0.5		
Lip Balm, Chap Stick	10	0.4	14	0.5
Eye Drops, 0.05 fl oz	8	0.3		
Toothbrush, short	7	0.2		
Manual Razor	13	0.5	5	0.2
Total Toiletries		**8.3**		**13.8**

Electronics	Shawn (g)	Shawn (oz)	Bob (g)	Bob (oz)
Tablet: 7" Google Nexus with case	405	14.3	401	14.1
Keyboard: folding, bluetooth	249	8.8		
Battery pack: 10,400 mAh with case	235	8.3	235	8.3
Phone / Camera: Moto G with case	166	5.9	144	5.1
AC Adapter and Cables	84	3.0	90	3.2
Total Electronics		**40.2**		**30.7**

Shelter and Sleeping	Shawn (g)	Shawn (oz)	Bob (g)	Bob (oz)
Tent, Cuben Fiber, 8 stakes, bags, pole	411	14.5		
Sleeping Bag, down quilt, Jacks R Better	578	20.4	658	23.2
Sleeping Pad, Klymit Inertia X Frame, inflatable	255	9.0	286	10.1
Ground Cloth, polycro, trimmed for tent	74	2.6		
Total Shelter and Sleeping		46.5		33.3

Cooking	Shawn (g)	Shawn (oz)	Bob (g)	Bob (oz)
Stove Kit, alcohol stove, wind screen, etc.			46	1.6
Fuel Bottle, 12 oz denatured alcohol			321	11.3
Cook Pot, 0.7L aluminum with lid			108	3.8
Bandana (pot holder)			31	1.1
Water Bottle, extra, not on bike, 1L platypus	24	0.8	24	0.8
Plastic Cup, small, 10 oz (2 total)			28	1.0
Matches (30 pcs minimum)			13	0.5
Utensil, spork, Light My Fire (2 total)			20	0.7
Can Opener			8	0.3
Water Purification, MicroPur tablets (16)			13	0.5
Total Cooking		0.8		21.6

GRAND TOTALS		Shawn		Bob
	Pounds	11.8		10.6

Bicycle Related Items

Bicycle - The actual model or brand selection will be left up to the reader. My steel frame touring bike cost less than $1500, and the bicycle performed extremely well. Although heavier than a regular road bike, the durability of the touring bike was worthwhile. My strong advice would be to purchase, break in, and use a Brooks B-17 saddle. I was skeptical and did not change to this saddle until a few weeks into our trip, but it was well worth it.

Fenders - These could be optional. I installed fenders, but my riding partner did not. We both made it fine. I did experience less water, dirt, and grit being thrown onto my shoes, chain, and panniers. The fenders do add a slight amount of weight. Since I also use this bicycle for commuting, to me they were worth having.

Headlight - This item was more valuable than I would have expected. I would recommend a 300 lumen or higher light. It can also be detached and used as a flashlight if camping. Even though we rode very little after dark, the main advantage was using it in flash mode during the day. Cars ahead could see us more easily, and often shifted right to allow cars trying to pass us from behind more room. I highly recommend using a headlight on flash mode at all times. Do some research to find a model that has enough battery life to run for multiple days on flash or strobe mode. The Cateye Volt 300 would last four or more days when flashing. Other brands likely have a similar model, but look carefully. Bob tried two different headlights, but neither would last an entire day.

Tail Light - Again, this is very helpful, even during the day. I recommend a model that can run multiple days on a charge. I used mine on flash mode all the time during the ride. It made me much more visible to approaching traffic.

Pump - This piece of gear is obviously necessary. The rolling resistance of tires is less at higher pressures. I would pump our tires back up to the recommended pressure every two or three days. Also, we needed a pump to fix any flats. In our case, neither pump failed, but a quality pump is preferred over a cheap one. Pumps with a short section of hose will apply less stress to the valve stem than those models that attach directly to the stem.

Computer - Everyone seems to have a favorite bike computer. I prefer a wired version, since it is simpler and only requires one battery. One battery did last for the entire two month trip. I like to be able to see speed, daily distance, and time. Just about any model will suffice, so select whatever works best for you.

Panniers - We saw all kinds of panniers and bags as we met other cyclists. I was completely satisfied with our Arkel Dry Lites. They weighed about a pound for the pair, and they cost under $100. Other heavy duty large panniers will weigh as much as 5 pounds. If you plan to travel light, the Arkel panniers will hold just enough gear to work well. They still look good and do not show any signs of wear, even after constant exposure to the elements during our two month trip.

Additional Bag - I found that a handle bar bag worked great for me as an additional bag. It had a clear map sleeve on top, and conveniently held sunglasses, snacks, a wallet, a cable lock and key, and a few other small items. My medium bag weighed about a pound and was attached with Velcro and shock cords. This was a lighter option than larger bags with a metal frame or that need a bracket for mounting. My friend used a trunk bag on top of his rear rack instead. This seemed to work for him. Either way, the supplemental bag kept small items easily within reach at breaks, so we did not have to open up the panniers each time we stopped.

Water bottles - I carried two 28 ounce bottles, and I wrapped about three feet of duct tape around each one. Duct tape has many uses. These two bottles were sufficient for all but a few days when services were very far apart. I did carry an additional 32 ounce or 1 liter collapsible bottle which is described later.

Flag and pole - This item is certainly optional and a matter of personal preference. My tent needed one pole for the front. I was able to make a tube mount for this pole, and then attach flags to the top of it. I sewed a black fabric sleeve to fit over the top of the pole, and then sewed three flags to this sleeve. I chose small American, Oklahoma, and Christian flags for my ride. It was a nice conversation starter, and I felt like it made me slightly more visible to motorists. An added benefit was that we could easily determine the wind direction by observing the flags during a rest stop!

Arkel Dry Lites – these super light panniers are large pockets with a folding, dry bag style top. They performed great!

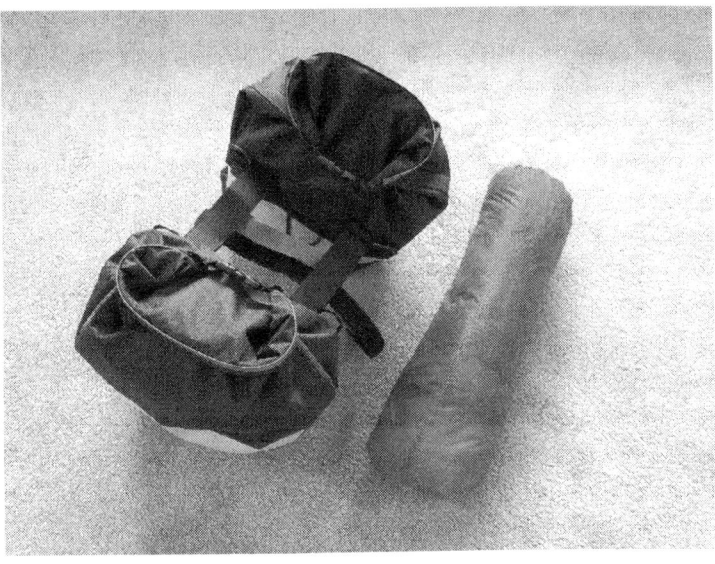

This is ALL of my gear. Panniers and one long blue bag with our tent and ground cloth. We were very light and did not regret it.

Clothing

Shoes - I chose cleated mountain bike style shoes. The cleats are recessed, so walking in them after riding was not awkward. They were similar to hiking shoes, and they ended up being quite comfortable. It would have been possible to only take this one pair of shoes for the entire trip. My friend wore tennis shoes and had standard pedals, and this one pair of shoes worked fine for him. So, a tour can be done with only one pair of shoes.

Bike Shorts - I have several pairs, but I chose the most comfortable pair to take on the tour. Only one pair of shorts are needed for a tour, and I washed mine nearly every night. I will describe my laundry procedure later. I initially planned to take two sets of bike clothes, but one set worked fine.

Bike Shirt - This could be a true jersey, or in my case a fitted T shirt worked well. The fabric should be of the quick dry, synthetic type. I recommend a bright color. I used neon lime green for the first month and this was my only short sleeve shirt that I carried. It was also washed out each night. During the second half of the tour when it was warmer, I added a short sleeve bright orange shirt and alternated shirts. I could use one shirt to ride in and then wear the other shirt in town after showering. Many other cyclists that we encountered were wearing dark colors. They were very difficult to see. The bright colors are much more visible and therefore safer, even during the day.

Bike Gloves - This is another item that needs to fit comfortably. Find a pair that you like with ample palm padding. Most of the time I wore these fingerless gloves, but I did use full finger winter gloves on cold mornings.

Socks - Again, the synthetic quick dry type are essential. Synthetic fabrics will dry much more quickly than cotton. Two pair of these will work for the entire tour. I would wash a pair each night, and put on the dry pair to wear the next day. This worked very well. I did not have a single blister using these synthetic socks.

Helmet - This essential item seems obvious, but we did encounter several riders not wearing helmets. I prefer the style with a sun visor, but select the type that fits and works well for you. I also highly recommend a helmet mounted mirror. In fact, I would consider it a necessary item. More on that later.

Long Sleeve Shirt - This item is also synthetic material and quick dry. It could be used as a base layer under my bicycle shirt on cold mornings. It could also be worn to sleep in if camping in cold weather. I used it most in the evenings after riding.

I would wash out my bicycle shirt and put on this shirt for the rest of the day. It could also be worn around camp or out to dinner.

Long Pants - These were the lightweight, quick dry, convertible style. If camping, they could be slept in for added warmth. I also wore them to ride in on the coldest mornings. Later during the tour, I zipped off the legs and converted them to shorts. I would wear them in the evenings after riding, since I usually washed out my bike shorts each day.

Underwear - I did carry one pair of synthetic standard briefs. These were worn after riding under pants or shorts. The quick dry fabric would dry quickly after washing.

Rain Jacket - This item is a lightweight, mostly waterproof long sleeve jacket. It provides some rain protection, although not many fabrics can stop an all-day rain. It also can be worn on the coldest mornings. I wore it in the evenings, if needed, which could be around camp or out to eat.

Rain Pants - These turned out to not really be needed on my ride. They could be more useful if camping most nights. If staying in motels, I would leave them at home. I found that riding in the rain wearing just bicycle shorts was comfortable - no rain pants were needed, even in colder temperatures.

Alternate Footwear - I carried an extremely lightweight pair of sandals, more like flip flops. They were not necessary, but I did wear them around town a few days. They also came in handy a few times to wear in showers that did not look very clean. These may be an optional item for some.

Down Vest - This ultralight down vest was only used a few times. I would carry an equivalent item if camping, but it was not needed if staying in motels or hotels.

Base Layer Top - I carried this long sleeve, silk base layer during the first half of the tour. It was used on cold mornings under other layers of clothing. I would consider it essential if camping.

Fleece Cap - This was a synthetic lightweight fleece beanie style hat. It is only needed if camping. This cap will keep in much of your body heat when sleeping outside in cold weather. It is not needed if staying in hotels or motels, so I did not use it much at all. I ended up sending it back with my wife after two weeks.

Balaclava - This thin head covering will fit under a helmet. If I had to carry only one item of head gear, this balaclava would be it. I wore it many times on cold mornings to keep my head and ears warm. It may also be possible to only use this head gear if camping, but that may depend on the individual.

Leggings - These bicycle leggings were very useful to wear with bicycle shorts on the cold mornings. I did not use them during the second half of the trip as the days warmed up. Honestly, I accidentally left them at a rest stop. Be sure to look around for all of your gear when leaving those rest stops!

Sleeves - These are similar to leggings, but for arms. I often wore these along with a bicycle shirt on colder mornings. They can also be worn under other long sleeve layers when it is extremely cold. I often wore the sleeves after I had removed other layers, since they could easily be peeled off as it warmed up.

Warm Gloves - These were full fingered bicycle gloves with some palm padding. They were very nice on cold mornings. As it warmed up, I would change to the other fingerless gloves. These could be worn for extra warmth around camp when camping.

Head Band - I had purchased and carried a lightweight synthetic head band. This could be used to cover my ears on cool mornings. As it turned out, I rarely used it. If it was cool enough, the balaclava was fine. If it warmed up too much for the balaclava, the ear band was not needed. I would not recommend carrying this item.

Helmet Cover - This was another item that I did not need. This cover was windproof and water resistant. I only ended up wearing it a few days. The balaclava provided enough warmth on cold days. I suppose it may have been more useful if we had ridden in many days of rain. The rain we did experience did not seem to soak my head, and the helmet cover would get warm since it was not breathable.

Socks – I did carry two extra pairs of socks, although I dropped one pair for the last part of the ride and just used two pairs total. I would wash one pair at night, and wear the clean and dry pair the next day.

Glasses – I wear prescription glasses, so I carried that pair while I wore prescription cycling sunglasses. These had a lens that wrapped slightly on each side, and this was very convenient for blocking debris and light rain from my eyes and face.

Biking clothes, one set. These clothes were washed out each evening and were dry by the next day.

Additional clothing items, and non-biking clothing. Some of these items were not needed and sent back.

Lightweight Bicycle Touring

Miscellaneous

Bicycle Repair - This kit contained the following: one spare tire, two spare tubes, tube patch kit, tire irons, multi-tool, chain oil, rags, extra chain link, zip ties, spare bolts, and tiny pliers. We did not need the spare tire, but if we had sliced a tire on the road, the spare would have been necessary. I only ending up needing one of the tubes, but two at a time should be enough. You can always purchase more supplies on the road or have a package sent to yourself via general delivery. The patch kit took care of most of our flats. I prefer the glued variety, rather than the peel and stick type. Two tire irons will work, and we removed the entire tire to fix our flats - this worked much better than leaving the tire half way on the rim. Be sure that your multi-tool or tool kit will fit every bolt, screw, and nut on your bicycle. I carried chain lubricant and rags and would oil the chain every few days. The extra chain link was not needed, but was cheap and lightweight insurance in case a chain broke. Zip ties are light and have many uses. I had some spare bolts like those used to attach the rack or fenders, so I carried a few of them. I was not sure about the tiny pliers before the trip, but they proved to be extremely useful to remove small wires in our tires from steel belted tire debris.

Bike Lock - I opted for a braided steel cable and a padlock for security. I would lock the bikes together whenever we went into a store or restaurant. The cable was small in diameter, but we figured that not many people would have cable cutters in their pocket. We often parked our bikes within sight, but this lightweight solution provided some peace of mind.

Dog Repellant - I carried one small can of Halt dog repellant. It turned out to not be needed, but you never know. This was another lightweight item for insurance. We did meet another pair of riders that had a dog encounter resulting in a fall and a serious injury. It could be that repellant might have prevented this accident.

Knife - A small, lightweight pocket knife has many uses. I have used it to open packages, cut string, etc. This item is carried on a small ring with my lock key, safety whistle, and micro light.

Whistle - This is a small, orange, lightweight plastic whistle. Normally carried when backpacking, it can be useful if lost or in distress.

Wallet - I carried my money, credit cards and identification in a small lightweight wallet. This was kept in a Ziploc plastic bag with my emergency contact information.

Maps - I carried *Adventure Cycling Association* maps for a few sections, but I also carried maps for portions of our ride that were not on the Southern Tier. For these sections, I highlighted the route on state maps, and then cut out only the strip with our route. The maps would fit in my map sleeve on the handlebar bag, and all of them were kept in a gallon Ziploc to prevent them from being damaged or wet when not being viewed.

Paper and Pencil - I carried a few note sized pieces of paper along with a pencil in a Ziploc bag. This is handy for writing down notes for the day, phone numbers, directions, or anything else that needs to be quickly recorded.

Additional Miscellaneous if Camping

Quick Dry Towel - For camping, I would include a synthetic quick dry towel. These smaller towels are absorbent, but dry quickly. If showering at motels or hotels, then it is not needed.

Hand Sanitizer - For camping, hand washing can be difficult. I carry a 2 ounce bottle of hand sanitizer to use before meals. It can also be used as an emergency fire starter, since it is primarily alcohol.

Bug Repellant - When camping, especially as it gets warmer, some kind of bug repellant may be helpful. I carry small quantities, since more can be purchased at towns along the route.

Micro Light - This item may not be necessary if carrying a bicycle headlight, but it can be convenient for finding things in a tent at night, or looking in bags after dark. It is a small, keychain sized light, and I carried it on a ring with my knife, whistle, and cable lock key.

Small Rope - This can be used to lash your tent or another equipment bag to your rear rack. It can also be used as a clothes line for wet or washed clothes. The rope can be used to hang a food bag if camping in bear country, and it can be used to make some emergency repairs.

First Aid

First Aid Kit - My homemade kit contained: a needle and sewing thread, safety pins, antibiotic ointment, sting relief gel, alcohol pads, band aids, throat lozenges, decongestant tablets, antihistamine tablets, anti-acid tablets, Imodium, Pepto tablets, 2x3 gauze pads, and body glide (anti-friction for blisters). This kit was perfect for me, but your items may vary. If riding through towns frequently, most of these items can be picked up during the tour if needed, but some should be on hand for emergencies.

Nail Trimmers - Since I was on the road two months, these were needed several times. I carried a small, lightweight pair. They can also be used to cut small line or tape.

Tweezers - These are useful for removing splinters or other foreign objects from fingers or toes. They can also be used to pull thorns from tires.

Ear Plugs - These might be needed if you are riding with someone who makes some noise while sleeping. They may also be needed if camping and the tree frogs are being excessively noisy. I include them here because I carried them in my first aid kit bag.

Toiletries or Personal Hygiene

Vitamins / Medications / Ibuprofen - Select the appropriate items for your trip or situation. I only needed Ibuprofen for the days my knees were more sore than usual.

Soap - The most convenient option for my ride was a 2 ounce plastic bottle of liquid peppermint soap. This was only needed occasionally. More would be needed if camping, but less if staying in motels or hotels.

Sunscreen - This was needed on exposed skin. I preferred to carry a smaller sized container, and then refill or purchase more as needed. One location not expected to need sunscreen was areas of my forehead exposed by ventilation holes in my helmet. I will tell you that you should have a great tan, in some areas, after a two month tour!

Toilet Paper - Again, carry more if camping, and less if in hotels or motels. It is still nice to have a quantity of this on hand if needed when out on the highway away from towns. It is not too difficult in many areas to dig into the ground a few inches with the heel of a shoe, and then bury and cover everything before departing. "Leave no trace" philosophies apply here.

Toothpaste - A small tube is plenty for several weeks, and then a new quantity can be purchased.

Floss - A small container is enough for a few weeks, and like other items, more can be purchased along the route.

Lip Balm - Chap Stick or other brands help to prevent chapped lips and a product with sunscreen might be desirable.

Eye Drops - These are not needed by everyone, but try to carry the smallest bottle available if you need them.

Toothbrush - Carry your preferred brand and type, but I cut off several inches of the handle. It will fit better in a Ziploc bag, and it reduces weight. Yes, I am that particular about reducing gear weight!

Manual Razor - You can carry your favorite brand, or the lightest version you can find works fine. It depends on the person, but one disposable razor lasted for all of my two month tour. I used soap when available and did not carry shaving cream.

Miscellaneous items including the bike took kit, lock and cable, dog repellant, wallet, maps, pencil, paper, and tie down rope.

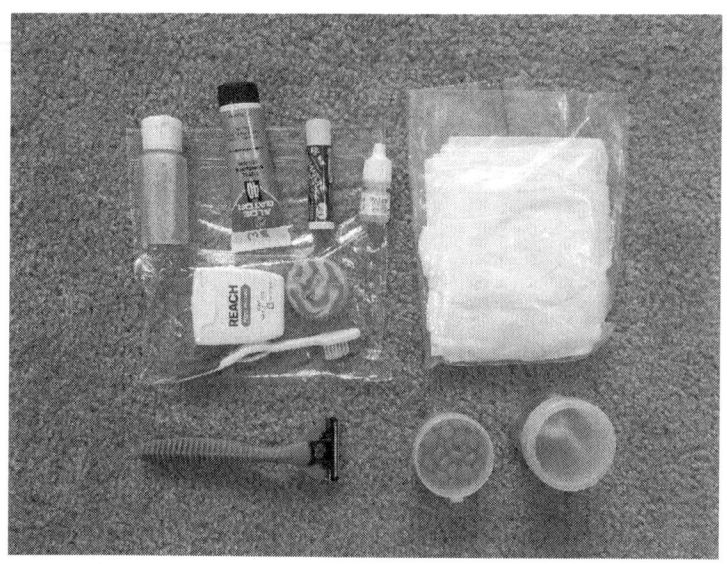

Personal hygiene items.

Electronics

Tablet - This was my preferred and primary device. I used it to journal my trip, access the internet, check email, send photos, etc. I opted for a small 7 inch tablet, since it was lighter than a larger tablet. It also fit into my bags well, and was convenient to carry into stops along the route. I kept it in a protective case, and then put that into a gallon Ziploc bag.

Keyboard - For journaling, I found a keyboard very convenient for my hour or more of writing each evening. This may not be necessary for many. My folding model connected via Bluetooth to my tablet. It worked very well, and was small and convenient. The rechargeable battery lasted for days.

Battery Pack - Since we intended to camp most nights, I carried a rechargeable battery pack. This 10,400 mAh unit would charge my phone or tablet three or four times before the pack needed to be recharged. As we decided to stay in hotels and motels, the battery pack was not needed. I sent it back home about half way through our trip. For camping, it would allow us to not need electricity for several days at a time. This pack could be used to charge my tablet, keyboard, phone, headlight, and tail light. We did investigate solar power, but most of my research indicated that the solar panels currently available, in a size small enough for biking, are simply not powerful enough to fully charge a tablet during the daylight hours.

Phone / Camera - Like most people, I am using my phone as my camera almost exclusively. I do have a larger, nicer camera at home, but for a tour, the camera phone worked very well.

AC Adapter and Cables - I only carried enough cables to charge two devices at a time. I carried an AC adapter with two USB plugs, and then two USB cables. They all fit nicely into a Ziploc bag.

Some riders may want to carry more or less electronics than I. Remember, these items do tend to weigh more for their size than other gear.

Electronics items, including a phone, tablet, battery pack, Bluetooth folding keyboard, and assorted cables.

All electronics packed in sealed freezer bags for protection from moisture.

Shelter and Sleeping

These items are needed if camping. I carried all of them, just in case, but ended up not using them.

Tent or Shelter - I carried a Cuben fiber single wall tent. This tent, along with titanium stakes, is extremely lightweight. Select a tent carefully, because this item can end up weighing many pounds and take up more volume than is available in small bags. I lashed it to the top of my rear rack.

Sleeping Bag - Down sleeping bags weigh less than synthetic bags, but they often require a larger investment. Down bags normally pack into a smaller space than synthetic bags. I have switched to a down quilt, made for backpacking, which weighs even less than a down sleeping bag. If camping, it may be a good option to purchase only a heavy enough bag to keep you warm when wearing all of your clothing in the bag.

Sleeping Pad - There are numerous options available as a sleeping pad. This can make hard ground considerably more comfortable. Be cautious of thicker pads, since they can weigh several pounds. I use a couple of inflatable options that weigh around 10 ounces.

Ground Cloth - This sheet of plastic can be used under a tent to protect the bottom. It can also be used as the only ground protection if camping under a tarp. The polycro style ground sheets are tough and very lightweight. This type of plastic can be purchased at home improvement stores as an insulating product to cover sliding glass doors. The type that shrinks slightly when heated is polycro. It was cut to exactly fit the tent footprint.

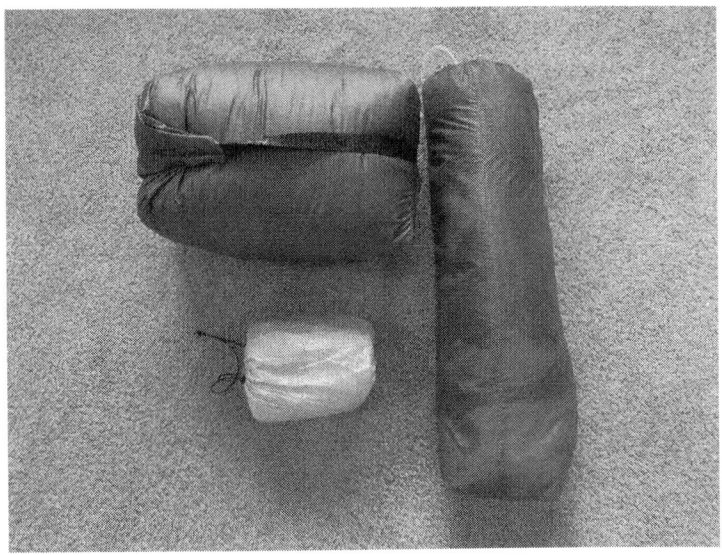

The sleeping quilt is in the dark green dry bag, the long blue bag contains the tent, stakes, and ground cloth, and the light green bag contains the inflatable sleeping pad.

The extremely lightweight tent and other gear setup for an overnight stay on a tour of the Katy Trail.

Cooking

These items may be needed if camping, and I did carry most of them during our tour.

Stove Kit - A lightweight stove can be used to heat water or cook meals when camping. My preferred type is an alcohol stove made out of an aluminum soda can. This extremely light stove can be handmade or found online.

Fuel Bottle - This is used to carry stove fuel - denatured alcohol. I usually carry a 12 ounce bottle of fuel, which is generally enough to boil 24 cups of water.

Cook Pot - A 0.7 liter aluminum pot with a lid will hold 2 cups of water with room to spare. This lightweight cook container is also large enough to hold my stove, bandana, matches, and water treatment tablets for transport.

Bandana - This item can be used as a pot holder to pick up a hot pan. It can be used as a large bandage in emergencies, and was wrapped around my stove and other items for packing into my cook pot.

Water Bottle (Extra) - For longer dry stretches of the route, I carried a one liter collapsible bottle. This could be filled and packed into my panniers for hotter or drier sections of my route. One liter bottles of water could also be purchased along the route before dry stretches.

Plastic Cup - A small, plastic cup has several uses. If the one cup level is marked on the cup with a permanent marker, it can be used to measure quantities of water for boiling. It can hold coffee, hot chocolate, or other beverages while traveling. I have used my cup in motel microwave ovens to heat water for tea or coffee. It also can be used to find holes in tubes - more on that later.

Matches - A small box of 30 or so matches can be carried in a plastic bag, and then packed in the cook pot. These are used to light the alcohol stove or start a campfire in an emergency.

Utensils - I only needed to carry one utensil, and that was a spork. This plastic camping utensil has a spoon on one end and a fork on the other. This, along with a pocket knife, should be sufficient to prepare and eat meals when camping.

Can Opener - The small, army style, keyring sized can openers are lightweight and can open cans when touring. If you purchase canned food with pull type lids, it may not be needed. We did not need it for our trip. I would also recommend that you avoid carrying heavy canned foods.

Water Purification - When camping, it is necessary to be able to purify water for drinking. Water that is boiled does not need normally need to be treated. I carried MicroPur tablets, but there are other options. If staying in motels or hotels, water purification tablets may not be needed. I was happy to carry a small quantity, since the tablets are very lightweight. For camping, you can also carry filters, but these tend to be much heavier. The best purification option may depend on the route and area of the world being traveled.

Cooking items, including stove kit, fuel bottle, cook pot, bandana, cups, sporks, matches, water treatment tablets, can opener.

All cooking items packed into a single mesh bag.

The alcohol stove in action, boiling water for meals on a tour of the Katy Trail.

Close up of the alcohol (soda can) stove in action – extremely light and boils water quickly.

Resupply Box

I also put together a resupply box. This box was left at home with my wife. It contained items that she could ship to me, or that she would bring in the car on the few times that she came out to meet us.

Items carried in the resupply box included the following:

Spare tires
Spare tubes
Hand sanitizer
Toilet paper
Soap
First aid supplies
Shoe cleats
Brake pads
Stove fuel
Razors
Matches
Water treatment tablets
Tube patches
Vitamins/Ibuprofen
Duct tape
Battery for micro light and computer
Air mattress patch
Laundry soap
Extra info cards
Ziploc bags - quart freezer

Additional Gear Recommendations

I would like to elaborate on a few gear items specific to the bicycle.

<u>Seat or Saddle</u>

Before my tour, I researched for hours about seats and saddles. I had a seat on my bike with what I thought to be good padding. I had heard of leather saddles, but I just was not convinced that a suspended piece of leather could be more comfortable. My riding partner had a much harder seat, and within a week of starting the tour he had saddle sores and was in quite a bit of pain. After more reading and a few suggestions by friends, we both purchased new saddles about two weeks into our trip. We opted for the Brooks B-17 leather saddles and purchased the Proofide treatment to help break them in. I could tell a huge difference within two days. It simply does not look like it should be comfortable, but I can assure you that it is. I plan to keep that seat for the rest of my life. My best explanation for how it works is that the leather will give, stretch slightly, and form to your personal backside. The pressure points that start to hurt on other seats stretch the leather in that area. It feels like the pressure when sitting is evenly distributed, and no single point or points are bearing most of the weight.

<u>Rear View Mirror</u>

After a two month tour, I cannot imagine riding without a helmet mounted rear view mirror. I have seen others with bike mounted mirrors and eyeglass mounted mirrors. For me, the helmet mounted mirror could be adjusted so that I could see traffic behind me without moving my head or taking my eyes off the road. I felt that it was crucial when riding on narrow sections or stretches without a shoulder to be able to watch approaching cars as they neared me. If I felt like they were not giving enough space, then I could shift right or even roll off into the grass if necessary. If I was on a curve, or I needed to see cars that were not directly behind me, then I could turn my head with the helmet mounted mirror and see slightly to either side. This is simply not possible with a bike or handlebar mounted mirror. In fact, I got so used to the mirror, that for weeks later, I found myself glancing up to look in the mirror when walking down the street to check on a noise that I heard behind me. Find a good, rear view, helmet mounted mirror and install it before your next long ride. I think you will like it.

Brooks B-17 leather saddle.

Rear view mirror – rider's view.

Water Topics

In cooler weather, the following suggestions may not be necessary. I found them to be very useful in warmer weather.

In cooler weather, I carried both full water bottles in cages on my bicycle frame. As the weather warmed, my second bottle would get quite warm late in the morning. As temperatures warmed even more, my water would not stay cool for long.

If you are staying in motels or hotels, you can fill those water bottles in the evening after a ride. Many lodging options have a refrigerator in the room. I would often put my second (or third) bottle in the freezer and let it freeze overnight. I would take the other first bottle and fill it full of ice from the ice machine, and then fill the rest of the bottle with cold water.

Before heading out on a warm day, I would pack all three bottles into my panniers. At my water breaks, I would pull one out for a drink, and then pack it back in the bag. This kept my water much cooler during the day. Often, there would still be a piece of ice in the bottle that started out as frozen in the morning.

When stopping for lunch or at a location where water was available, I would refill my bottles. The cold water or ice already in the bottles would cool down any new water, and keeping them in a bag would keep the water from getting extremely warm during the day.

Experiment with this type of method to see what might work best for your ride. We also would fill bottles with ice and then top them off with Gatorade or another sports drink once per day or every two days. This helped to replace some of the salts and minerals that we were sweating out on warm days.

Clothes Washing

Most of the time, we did not find a laundry facility that was convenient during the ride. Laundry facilities were used a few times on rest days, but this was not very often. My method of washing clothes was found by trial and error, and it ended up working very well for me during the tour.

I wanted to wash my riding clothes each day, or almost every day. Some days they were dirtier than others, but it was nice to start with fresh clothes each morning. The washing method that I used was convenient, quick, and easy to do each evening.

Since we were in hotels or motels each night, this method worked nicely. Camping tourers may have to work out a slightly different solution.

Each evening, I would take a shower after the ride before eating dinner. I would actually get into the shower wearing all of my riding clothes - shirt, shorts, and socks. I would use bar soap to wash the clothes while they were still on me - just like normal showering. As I washed a piece of clothing, I would pull it off and drop it in the bottom of the shower and stand on it. Once all of the clothes had been washed, they would be in the shower under my feet. As I then started to shower normally, I would march around and stomp on the clothes on the shower floor. They would be rinsed continuously with soapy water and clean water while I walked all over them. You may laugh, but this worked!

Once I was finished with my normal shower, I would pick up one item of clothing at a time and rinse it several times under the shower head. Since all of my riding clothes were synthetic, quick dry fabrics, they could be twisted and wrung out thoroughly. After each item was rinsed and wrung out, I would hang it over the shower rod. After shutting off the water, before using a towel on myself, I would take each item of clothing, roll it in the towel, and then wring it again while in the towel. I found that my synthetic fabrics were extremely dry at the end of this process. I then would hang each item on a hanger in the room, and they were all dry by the next morning. If I could hang them in front of the air conditioner fan, that would speed the drying process. I was surprised at how fresh the clothes smelled and how clean they seemed after this washing process each evening.

Cleaning Chains

I found that my chain needed to be cleaned about every ten days or so. The chain would need to be cleaned more frequently after riding in a day or two of rain or drizzle. There are several products that can be purchased and carried to clean a chain. I did not want to carry these items due to the additional weight. Brushes can be used, but the oily spray from trying to scrub with a small brush seems to go everywhere and on everything. The first cleaning job on our tour was done with a spray chain cleaner from a bike shop, but this product was costly.

The best, most cost effective product for cleaning chains turned out to be brake cleaner from an auto parts store. This product was available at most towns, and it worked very well. I would lean the bike over against something to the right side. This would allow me to turn the crank and spray the chain with cleaner as the chain moved slowly. With the bike tilted right, the over spray and dirt being removed would not get onto my tire or rim. The pressure of the brake cleaner spray would blast off dirt, grit, and grime from the chain. Once the chain is sufficiently clean, apply a generous coat of chain lubricant to each chain link.

There may be other methods, but for me, this method was convenient to use while touring. Even with over 3,000 miles on my chain, it is still performing very well. We did not experience any chain breaks or drive train issues during the tour.

Fixing Flats

This would seem like a simple task. I have seen it demonstrated many times, and even done it numerous times myself. The normal method is to pry one side of the tire over the edge of the rim, pull out the leaking tube, replace or fix the tube, and tuck it back in between the tire and rim.

My concern with this method was that I could never be sure that my tube was not pinched or in a bind somewhere. It was also more difficult to check the inside of the tire for thorns with it still on the rim. After a couple of flats, we ended up settling on a method that worked well for us.

First, it really helps if the tire label is lined up with the valve stem. This helps you to know where on the tire to look for a thorn or wire, after finding a hole in the tube. If possible, align your tire labels with each valve stem before starting a long tour.

Upon discovering a flat or leaking tire, we would pull over in a safe location and remove the wheel. For the back tire, it is much easier on my bike if you can turn the bike over and rest it upside down on the seat and handlebars. I do have to remove my light and computer before resting it on the ground this way. Before removing a tire from the rim, find some way to mark the tire and rim to know how they were lined up with each other. Once the wheel is removed, the tire irons can be used to carefully pry one side of the tire off of the rim. With one bead off of the trim, I was able to roll the other edge of the tire off of the trim by hand. A tire bead is the term for the edge of a tire that sits on the wheel. Even if tire irons are needed, completely remove the tire and tube from the rim as one unit.

Again, be sure that you have marked the tire and rim or tire and tube to know how they were aligned with each other. Carefully pull the tube out of the rim. If possible, I prefer to find the hole and fix it on the side of the road. I know that some want to throw in a new tube and get back on the road. The problem with that method is that if you do not know where the hole is located, then you do not know where on the tire to inspect for some sharp object. Some of the steel belted tire debris wires can be hard to locate.

I have found that the plastic cup can be easily used to find a hole in a tube. I take my small plastic drinking cup and fill it about 2/3 with water from a water bottle. Then, inflate the tube slightly with a pump. Fold sections of the tube, insert into the cup of water, and look for bubbles. If none are found, pull it out, fold it again slightly further along the tube, and reinsert it into the water. Repeat as necessary until you find the hole. This process is easier with two people, one to hold the cup, and one to work the tube. I have successfully used this method several times to find a hole while on the side of the road. It also uses very little water, less than 8 ounces.

After the hole, or holes, in the tube are found, it is important to locate the position of that hole as it compares to the tire. This process is much easier with the tire removed from the rim. I can stretch it open and look and feel for any thorn or wire that may be in my tire. I do have to be careful to not cut myself on any object in the tire. Many times, whatever object pierced the tube is still lodged in the tire. The pliers or tweezers can be helpful to pull out any object that is found. I cannot stress how important it is to be sure that any sharp object is found or removed from the tire. Otherwise, you may be fixing another flat very soon. Since the tube can be flipped 180 degrees within the tire, you may need to check the tire on the opposite side of the valve stem for an embedded object.

After the tube is patched or replaced, the tube can be pumped up slightly until it is able to hold its shape. Now, take the tube and tuck it into the tire that is still off of the rim. With the tube now in the tire, I take the valve stem and insert it into the rim. By hand, I then work one side of the tire over one edge of the trim. Once one tire bead is on the rim, I then, by hand, work the other tire side over the rim. Normally, I can remount the tire without the use of any tire irons or tools that might damage the tube.

The tire can now be fully inflated and the wheel remounted. This may not work best for everyone, but the method proved to work very well for me during the tour. I hope these suggestions improve the ability of at least some to deal with the inevitable flat tires. I found that I could remove the tire and tube, fix the leak, and have it all remounted in about twenty minutes or so.

Using a cup to find a hole, and using very little water to do it!

Rotating my tires, the back tire was wearing thin by the end of the trip.

Directions and Distances

Many times on our tour we would ask other people about distances to certain points or places. Be very aware, most non-bicyclists do a very poor job of estimating distances. On several occasions, we asked about the distance to a water stop, convenience store, or other landmark. We found that people who only travel by car tend to drastically under estimate distances. Often this is just an inconvenience, but if you are needing water or food, it can be frustrating and concerning to those of us traveling at only 10 to 12 miles per hour.

Another thing to be cautious of is distances on billboards along highways. We have seen a few restaurants advertise "only five miles ahead" and then discover that they may have been stretching the truth. Five miles versus ten miles by car may not be too noticeable, but for a bicyclist this could really have an impact.

Be cautious when using distances provided by sources that are potentially less than accurate.

Riding the Shoulder

Many times, riding on the shoulder is the safest option when touring. The main concern for me when riding the shoulder is trash and debris. Traffic tends to knock any trash off and out of the road, but much of it comes to rest on the shoulder. This requires more attentiveness on the part of the cyclist to watch for and avoid shoulder debris, especially large items that may pose a significant hazard.

If traffic is extremely light, and a rear view mirror is being used, then I sometimes will ride in the right tire track on the road. By paying attention, I can easily move over onto the shoulder when traffic approaches from behind.

Now, the topic of rumble strips needs to be mentioned. Some states are more bike friendly than others, but I have seen every iteration of rumble strips along the shoulder. The best ones, if there is any such thing, have frequent gaps to allow bicyclists to move from the shoulder to the roadway and back. Just be prepared for the good, the bad, and the ugly.

Bridges pose an extra problem. Many times, the road will narrow across a bridge. This requires additional caution. Also, debris tends to accumulate even worse on bridges. The side rails of a bridge tend to reflect trash and debris back onto the bridge shoulder. It simply cannot escape the roadway.

You cannot be prepared for every shoulder obstacle, but perhaps this information will warn potential tourers and allow them to closely watch out for some of these hazards.

Some shoulders are better than others!

Other shoulders are starting to grow bumps of grass.

News and Television

One nice aspect of the tour was the vacation from news and television. Even though we stayed in motels each night, we only turned on a television twice, both times for a college basketball game - Go Sooners! I never watched the news or any other television during the tour, and this was extremely relaxing.

I think that we have an urge to know the news, much of which is not really news, and taking a two month break made it clear to me that most of the news we are fed is unnecessary. I know that we can waste a great deal of our time in front of a television or other devices, and the tour gave me a much welcome break.

Route Planning or Changing

Although we had tried to plan out the route as exactly as possible before the trip, detours were inevitable. One of the most frequent questions via journal comments or emails was that of how I did route planning and modifications.

We followed portions of the Southern Tier, but more than half of our route was self-guided. First, I started looking for state bicycle routes and maps. These were not very common. Georgia was the best state that we traversed in terms of publishing a decent bike route map. I did use recommended bicycle routes across southern Georgia highways.

Generally, I searched for highways with a shoulder. It did not seem to matter much if they were two lane or four lane, since the shoulder provided a safe place to ride. I initially routed without much care for distances between towns, but as we decided to stay in motels or hotels, I did have to make a few adjustments. Some of the distances between towns with any sort of lodging were too far apart on sections of the Southern Tier.

I found that many US highways, especially two lane versions with a shoulder, often had very light traffic. If an interstate was anywhere nearby, that seemed to draw away most through traffic. This was surprising to us, that a US highway could be so lightly travelled.

Before our trip, I used Google maps and street view to actually "look" at the road and determine if there was a shoulder of any sizeable width. This information is often not available on published paper maps. This same method was also used on the tour when trying to route a new segment. During the trip, we decided not to ride into Oklahoma, and I had not yet planned a route across northern Texas. With Google maps and street view, using the small tablet device, I could locate roads with a shoulder for this reroute. My only caution would be that sometimes road construction removes a shoulder in some areas. This was our experience north of Dallas, but it was only about half of a day with less than ideal riding conditions.

Another option that may help with routing in the west would be to use Warm Showers hosts or Adventure Cycling Association (ACA) route hosts. We did this on one occasion where the distance between services in the hot desert would have made for a difficult and long day. Also, if a hotel or motel does not seem available in a smaller town, search for a bed and breakfast or similar inn. This worked well for us in west Texas.

If you are camping, as we had initially planned to do, then you are able to be more flexible. Stealth camping, or camping in a hidden location, allows the bicycle tourer to stop between towns or services. The only added complexity is having to carry enough food or water to the camping location to provide for evening and morning needs.

Another way to check on routes and road quality is to search online bicycle touring forums. We used this information in a few locations to determine a better place to stay. We also used this information to completely skip a particularly dangerous tunnel along the Southern Tier route in Arizona.

Overall, I was very pleased with the roads and route selection. We did have some days with two lane roads and minimal shoulder, but some amount of that type of riding is difficult to avoid when traversing the country. Between the state paper maps, some state bicycle routes, the Southern Tier route, and Google street view, I was able to plot a very adequate route from coast to coast.

For daily navigation while riding, I would use a paper map, either the Southern Tier, or a state map cut down to size. On a few occasions, I copied turn by turn directions to paper from Google maps on days with multiple turns or more complex routing, but this was not very common. We did not use a GPS or phone while riding for navigation, other than the exception mentioned below.

One other option, on complex route days, is to use a mobile phone with Google maps bicycle navigation. Google maps will try to select bicycle friendly routes, but I would suggest spot checking the roads along your route using Google Street View to see whether the road has a good shoulder. With a single ear bud, you can let Google voice routing audibly provide turn by turn directions if your phone has enough battery capacity to last through the day. This method was used to navigate the Phoenix canal paths, and it worked very well. Most days though, the route was simple with few turns, so I only used the audio navigation a few times. I would rather keep the phone put away and enjoy the daily ride.

Some people have had decent success asking locals for directions or road suggestions. I would certainly beware of this, although it may work from time to time. As with distances, opinions vary widely. On US 90 in the southeast, we very much enjoyed that route. But in one town, a local resident told us to avoid it due to the narrow shoulder and heavy traffic. We did not have many other options, so we rode US 90 as planned. As it turned out, the road was fine, traffic was light, and the shoulder was wide. If possible, double check any suggestions made by non-bicyclist residents, even if they are trying to be helpful.

OUR JOURNEY

The following section is my daily blog or journal of the actual coast to coast ride in 2015. During this trip, I was able to learn and develop the suggestions and advice listed in the previous sections. We carried the exact gear listed in the earlier table, each having less than 12 pounds of gear, not including any food or water.

The Trip to Start the Trip

We left Tishomingo on a Friday morning just a few hours before several inches of snow began to fall in the area. Telling my wife goodbye was difficult, but I assured her it would only be about 2 1/2 weeks before she came and met us. The cold morning urged us to not linger long while loading the car. It was 20 degrees as we pulled out of the driveway. We had a full day of driving ahead of us on the way to Knoxville, Tennessee, to meet my friend Ron, who would shuttle us to the ocean.

The drive was uneventful, save the painful Memphis traffic. We had a tasty Subway sandwich for lunch along the way. We found a decent hotel about 500 miles down the road in Jackson, Tennessee. Since we needed two items we could not find before we left, we found our way to the local Target. Along with those items, we decided just to buy a few groceries for dinner was well. We would skip the crowded restaurants and dine in our hotel room. What is on the menu for a couple of guys on their own? My dinner consisted of Pad Thai, dried strawberries, lightly salted peanuts, and coconut water. For dessert, I had a banana nut muffin and coffee. Welcome to guys night out!

We planned to type a few notes, get a good night's rest, and take advantage of the free breakfast before we get an early start for Knoxville tomorrow morning. The adventure is ever closer.

The Night Before

We completed our trip to Knoxville and had a nice visit with Ron and his family on Saturday afternoon. The home cooked dinner was great. Today, Sunday, we loaded up the van, enjoyed worship at West Towne Christian Church, handed off my car keys to Steve in order to get it sold, and started our drive south.

We drove most of the day in fog and drizzle, leaving Tennessee and passing through North and South Carolina. We drove through Savannah as we entered Georgia, and then arrived at Brunswick to spend the night. This puts us about twenty minutes or so from Jekyll Island.

It is hard to believe, but Bob and I started discussing the possibility of this trip 16 months ago. We have talked about many possible adventures, including hiking the Appalachian Trail and canoeing the Mississippi River. The cross country bike tour has been his most desired adventure of the three. We spent some time discussing strategy, bikes, and gear, and purchased our touring bikes approximately 10 months ago. Once that was complete, we began to research and accumulate the necessary gear.

So here we are, everything in place and all of our best plans having been made. We are less than 12 hours from standing at the Atlantic Ocean, ready to ride west. It is quite surreal. We have been anticipating this for such a long time that tonight does not seem much different. I think it will really impact me tomorrow as we start pedaling away from the coast on our first day of the grand adventure.

We had a nice meal at the Ole Times Country Buffet. In fact, we arrived just before closing, but they let us in since it was before 8 PM. The nice cashier asked me if I wanted to see the buffet first, since "it was mostly soul food". Perhaps I did not look too ethnic to her? I told her that it was all good as we paid for our meals.

Ron's boys are playing cards in the hotel room as I type this entry. It is the same "oh bull" game that Ron and our friends played in high school. Some things never change.

That's all for today. Tomorrow is the real beginning.

Georgia

Day 1: March 2, 2015 - Jekyll Island to Waycross, GA - 62.1 miles

53 degrees to start, 74 degrees to finish, overcast then partly cloudy, wind SE at 3 mph, 8 AM to 3 PM, 12.2 average mph, 28 mph max, 5:05 hours riding time.

We spent last night in the Microtel in North Brunswick, Georgia. This put us about 15 miles by car from the ocean. Ron had our bikes on a rack on the back of his van for transport.

We drove out to Jekyll Island about 7:30 AM on Monday. Ron was able to get our bikes close to the ocean, but we walked the sidewalk and went out one of the boardwalks to get to the water. Construction prevented a straight shot out to the ocean, but it was still quite easy to access. We walked out and put our back tires in the water and took several ceremonial photos. The air was cool at the beach at 53 degrees. After our photos, Bob and I headed away from the beach, riding back toward the entrance to the island. The fog looked like smoke across the landscape as we pedaled past coastal marshlands.

I think our excitement was high because we seemed to pedal easily along at a good pace. All of those months of planning were now being put into action. We took turns, letting each of us lead part of the time as we rode single file back toward the mainland.

Traffic was light, but most of the ride had minimal shoulder space. Much of the shoulder was ruined by the rumble strip right down the middle of the shoulder. I will say that most all of the Georgia drivers did a good job of moving over to the inside lane to pass us. We watched our rear view mirrors closely to be safe, but no close calls happened. We ran both our rear lights (blinking red), and our front lights (blinking white). We maintained a good pace since the route stayed extremely flat for most of the day.

About 26 miles in, we stopped at a convenience store outside of Waynesville for a break and snacks. I purchased a banana and peanut M&Ms - perfect. A few patrons commented on it being a less than ideal biking day, but we were well visible and prepared.

By noon, we had ridden 40 miles and were in Nahunta. A quick Google search revealed that the Gold House Restaurant served a good hamburger. This was only half a mile off of our route, so we rode to the restaurant for an excellent cheeseburger and homemade French fries. The waitress mentioned that a few months ago she had served a couple biking from Florida to Canada, which apparently took eight months.

We were tired, but doing very well. The fog had lifted and temperatures were warming up after lunch. We took a rest break about 10 miles before Waycross. I called Ron to see what they had been doing. I figured that he would be about an hour from Waycross by car, and we were an hour from Waycross by bicycle. As we were discussing our plans, he drove up behind us on the shoulder. We decided that he would go on to Waycross for them to eat lunch, and then go investigate the Okefenokee Swamp Park to see if was something that we would want to do later that afternoon. My wife Jana had texted me after looking up information on the swamp park, and she thought it might be interesting.

Bob and I continued the ride to Waycross, feeling fatigued, but making it just fine. The interesting billboard of the day had this caption: "If your legs could talk..." I do not remember what it was advertising, but our legs certainly would have some things to say! We rode to the hotel and checked in around 3 PM. We stayed at the Baymont Inn & Suites in the middle of town, only a block off of our bike route. Since the Okefenokee Swamp Park closed at 5:30, Ron picked us up at the hotel and we drove out to take a swamp boat tour. Our guide, Ross, was very informative. He explained many aspects of the swamp and the wildlife and vegetation. We saw several alligators, and I certainly enjoyed the swamp tour. While on the tour, we were able to climb a large fire lookout tower to see the swamp from above. Those 107 steps were arduous after such a long ride! We were able to look at a few other exhibits at the Okefenokee Swamp Park before it closed. It would have been nice to have more of the day to see things, but we were glad that we could do a bit of sightseeing since Ron was available to drive us around. In future towns, we will not have this luxury.

The next priority for the tired bike riders was dinner. After some discussion, we decided that a Chinese buffet would be very tasty. We chose the New Beijing Buffet, and we were not disappointed. The selection was excellent, and we were able to fuel our engines for the second day of riding. The ice cream to top things off was just what this bicyclist needed.

So, we are back at the hotel, furiously trying to remember and type notes this evening. We will select the next day's destination and make our plans for the ride.

This was a fantastic starting day. It started cool and foggy, but ended warm and partly cloudy. The miles ticked away quickly across the flat terrain, and I enjoyed watching the swampland and large pine trees along the side of the road roll by.

Several large birds were sighted, and the traffic was tolerable. One day completed, about 49 days to go!

Back tires in the Atlantic Ocean, although the water just went out in this photo.

Departing Jekyll Island.

Day 2: March 3, 2015 - Waycross to Hahira, GA - 67.5 miles

60 degrees to start, 82 degrees to finish, overcast then partly cloudy, wind SSE at 4 to 7 mph, 8AM to 4PM, 12.1 average mph, 21 mph max, 5:35 hours riding time.

After breakfast at the hotel, we rolled out a few minutes after 8 AM. The forecast called for fog, but it was a perfect morning with great visibility. After winding our way toward the west end of Waycross, we headed out highway 122. Wow! This road was fantastic. The highway was only two lane with a minimal shoulder, but traffic was almost nonexistent. We pedaled easily along the flat highway, sometimes for more than a mile before a car headed west overtook us. The clouds broke, and it was a glorious morning for biking. The road did not have any services for about 40 miles, but we rode past berry farms, pine forests, swampy wetlands, and pecan orchards. Some of the houses looked like small plantations, and I wondered to myself if any of the families had been immigrants only a few generations back.

At 47 miles, we made it to Lakeland. My Subway foot long sandwich was consumed easily! The lunch break was very nice, and we lingered a bit longer than expected. This was a long morning, but lunch refreshed us and we headed west again. A few short rest breaks helped us persevere during the afternoon, including a billboard at one point with John Wayne quoting "I don't much like quitters, son".

After Lakeland, we rode past the Banks Lake National Wildlife Refuge. This large lake was filled with cypress trees, and looked more like an open swamp than a lake. The interesting thing that I noticed was all of the private property signs on small houses along the lake. Either they had a lease on the federal land, or the entire lake was not a refuge. After Lakeland, we also saw several military jets flying overhead, including a few A-10 Thunderbolts. I assumed that they were flying to or from Moody Air Force Base, which is southwest of Lakeland. I would also like to mention how courteous the Georgia drivers were on highway 122. Almost everyone moved completely over into the left lane as they passed us.

At Hahira, we made a quick stop in town to take a photo next to an old Southern Pacific caboose. This red bay window caboose was next to the main street and on our route. As we got back on the bikes, a young man named Matthew stopped to ask if he could ride with us for a mile or so on his way home. He explained that he was a junior, and 'might' be a senior next year. I encouraged him to keep his grades up and finish school. I also gave him one of my journal information cards. It was a great day, and we are not as tired as we had expected on the second long day. We have right at 130 miles of our journey behind us.

Ron picked us up after the ride to take us to the hotel. It has been great having Ron along for our trip these first few days. We really appreciate his willingness to help us get our adventure started.

After some discussion, google checking, and so forth, we decided to try the local Ole Times Country Buffet that the hotel clerk at the Econo Lodge had recommended. I will say that their selection was very good, and the $8.99 price was a good value. Buffets have worked well the last few days as we try to keep up with our rate of calorie burning.

Nice pine fields made for shady rest breaks.

Very light traffic on this road.

Day 3: March 4, 2015 - Hahira to Cairo, GA - 51.9 miles

62 degrees to start, 84 degrees to finish, overcast then partly cloudy, wind SSW at 5 to 15 mph, 8:30 AM to 3:30 PM, 10.5 average mph, 26 mph max, 4:55 hours riding time.

This was Ron's last day to tag along with us. We ate a good breakfast at the hotel, which included boiled eggs - excellent. I feel that a good dose of protein in the morning really helps my energy starting out. Ron dropped us off at the end of yesterday's ride, just west of I-75 at Hahira. We said goodbye, and thanks, for the extremely helpful shuttle service.

We continued on highway 122 heading west starting at 8:30 AM this morning. The road and traffic were very similar to yesterday. The two lane road had light traffic, but not much shoulder. Again, the Georgia drivers continue to impress me. Almost everyone gave us plenty of room, many slowed down, and several waved or gave us a 'thumbs up'.

Our route took us through Barney and Pavo towards Thomasville. We enjoyed cruising by pecan groves, one of which seemed to have 100 year old trees. We passed a couple of cotton fields and more live oak trees with Spanish moss.

The landscape was starting to become hillier, and the swamp areas were less frequent. As we biked along, many times the turtles that were sunning themselves on logs beside the road jumped into the water in the large ditches. Several times we surprised squirrels near the road and sent them running for cover into the woods.

There was more farmland on this leg of our journey, with many clean and tidy farmhouses beside the route. Several were complete with wooden rocking chairs on the front porches. A road with light traffic allows you to observe more of the scenery, which makes the trip more enjoyable. I also noticed that on Highway 122 there were few if any billboards. The lack of advertising was a welcome sight on such a scenic road.

As we neared Thomasville, Georgia, the traffic did become heavier. We thought that we might find a pizza eatery on the edge of town, but opted for the local Waffle House instead. My Philly steak and bacon melt was extremely tasty. As we were getting things back on our bikes after lunch, one of the Waffle House employees, Lois, asked us about our destination. She seemed quite interested after we explained that we were heading to California. I gave her one of my journal information cards.

We rode on US 84 around and west out of Thomasville. The road became four lane, and the traffic increased (as did the wind), but it was not too difficult to pedal up and down the rolling hills on our way to Cairo. The sun was out most of the time, so the temperature was rising into the low 80s.

We stopped at a store on the eastern edge of Cairo to pick up dinner ingredients - crunchy peanut butter and strawberry preserves for sandwiches. We have eaten out at restaurants the last few days, so a quiet and relaxing evening in the room will be enjoyable.

We arrived at the Best Western in Cairo around 3:30 PM. Craig at the front desk was very helpful and found a first floor room for us. This is very convenient since the bicycles are rolled into the room each night. This hotel was right along the route, and a good option for anyone riding this section.

Speaking of bicycles, they are performing admirably. So far, we have not had any flat tires, and the tires are holding pressure very well. The bikes seem to be very stable at higher speeds and are carrying the loaded bags without a problem.

We are three days and over 180 miles into our journey. Tomorrow's forecast is calling for rain so we will decide tonight on a plan. We could use tomorrow as a partial or full rest day, which would be very beneficial. Either way, we will post a journal entry tomorrow evening even if it turns out to be a full rest day.

Unique flower pots along the highway.

The Live Oaks with Spanish Moss were very nice to see.

Day 4: March 5, 2015 - Cairo to Bainbridge, GA - 26.4 miles

72 degrees to start, 78 degrees to finish, overcast then partly sunny, wind S at 4 to 8 mph, 9 AM to 12 PM, 10.4 average mph, 30 mph max, 2:30 hours riding time.

Many times rest days are dictated by the weather, and so it was with today. Each night we look at the route ahead, review weather, calculate distances to various destinations, factor in the wind speed and direction, and make a plan for the next day's distance and final destination.

Last night a front was expected to move through western Georgia today, and the rain chances went up drastically starting at 1 PM. We decided that we did not want to take the entire day off so we planned to use the morning for a shorter ride day. We hoped to beat the rain to Bainbridge. The forecast also mentioned a chance of morning fog before 9 AM. The 26 mile route from Cairo to Bainbridge would be a perfect distance for our 3 hour window this morning.

Before we left, I noticed that many areas on my tires, rims, and frame still had remnants of sand from the Atlantic Ocean. I took a few extra minutes this morning to wipe everything down and clean the wheels and frame. I also added a light coating of oil to the chain, just to make sure that it stayed well lubricated.

We departed from the Best Western in Cairo (pronounced Kay-Roe) after a decent free breakfast just after 9 AM. We had mapped out a rural route that would keep us off of the main highway. This was our first day off of the planned route. We had originally planned to angle southwest from Cairo to Chattahoochee, but that 50 mile distance would put us into the forecast period of rain.

It turns out that we were following the Georgia bike route 10 today. We left Cairo via Martin Luther King Jr and Collins Roads, which put us in Whigham after about 10 miles. We briefly joined US 84 through the quaint town before turning right onto Jowers Road which became Old Whigham Road. The route is only minimally longer than taking the main highway, but it was a wonderful detour.

The two lane road meandered around farmland, over gently rolling hills, with very light traffic. Once again drivers were extremely courteous and gave us plenty of room as they passed, even though there was not a shoulder to ride on. The road surface was reasonably smooth and in good condition. The morning clouds and south breeze kept us cool, but did not result in any head wind. Even after the clouds began to break, the temperatures before noon were only in the 70s.

Since we were only riding in the morning, we took it very easy, not wanting to push very hard, as shown by our average speed. We took a couple of rest breaks along the route, and late in the morning we ate our peanut butter and strawberry jelly sandwiches that we had prepared the night before.

It was a wonderful morning ride, and we rolled into the Holiday Inn Express hotel on the south side of Bainbridge just after noon. The check in time posted was 3 PM, but April at the front desk was very kind and had a room ready for us before 1 PM. This hotel was only about two blocks off of the route from Cairo to Chattahoochee, for anyone bicycling between those two towns. The location turned out to be great for us, and the rate using Hotwire.com was exceptional.

The remainder of the day was a rest day. I washed out clothes, worked on my journal, relaxed, and started planning the next day's ride. It began to rain at 2PM, so our morning only ride worked out perfectly. We are feeling quite well on day 4, and the partial rest day will really help us recover.

During the afternoon, I had my biking clothes soaking in the sink after washing them out. I had also washed my regular prescription glasses and was drying them with a hand towel. Well, one of the nose pads fell in the floor, which meant that the microscopic screw that held the pad in place was also missing. I looked all over the floor and counter, but simply could not find that tiny screw. I figured I would have to head to a drugstore after dinner to get a replacement. I went ahead and rinsed my biking clothes again and took them out of the sink, and then I let out the water. Much to my amazement, the tiny eyeglasses screw was resting in the bottom of the sink, right next to the drain. I could not believe it, but was quite happy to not have to make an extra trip to another store.

There were only a few places to eat within walking distance of the hotel, so we walked over to Zaxby's. This is a regional chain that serves chicken (fingers, wings, etc.), and is similar to an upscale KFC. The dinner plate I had included tenders, celery, fries, and boneless teriyaki wings - quite tasty.

I attempted to take a picture this morning to show the view of my helmet mounted mirror. This mirror has proved invaluable for watching approaching traffic. I highly suggest one, or something similar, for any cyclist. We are now 208 miles away from the Atlantic, still in Georgia, but we look forward to entering a new state, Florida, sometime tomorrow.

Following Georgia bike route 10.

Trying to show my mirror view to the folks back home.

Florida

Day 5: March 6, 2015 - Bainbridge, GA to Marianna, FL - 53.4 miles

A Day of Firsts

39 degrees to start, 46 degrees to finish, overcast, wind N at 5 to 10 mph, 8:30 AM to 3:30 PM (Eastern), 11.2 average mph, 38 mph max, 4:45 hours riding time.

Well, it can't be warm every day, and today was certainly NOT warm. The forecast last night said that it would be in the upper 40s before lunch and mid-50s in the afternoon, with some sun. Wrong. We had a great breakfast (omelets, sausage, fresh fruit, warm cinnamon rolls, and so forth), and when we rolled our bikes out of the front door of the hotel, we were greeted by the brisk 39 degree air! Today would be our *first* cold day.

We had dressed for the cold, including leggings, sleeves, base layer top, down vest under my bike jersey, full finger gloves, and a balaclava. It worked well, except for my fingers. They did get somewhat cold during the morning ride.

From Bainbridge we headed south on highway 97. This highway was a good section to ride. The shoulder was clear and wide enough, and the traffic level was quite minimal. The only stop for services that we saw was the Faceville Community Store. While waiting outside, a young man stopped to chat for a few minutes. He asked where we riding. I told him that we started at the Atlantic, and that we were ultimately headed to San Diego. He said "that's a long way...." to which I agreed.

We continued our ride south, enjoying the nice roads but having to climb a few hills along the way. At least one long incline slowed us to the pace of a snail, but we just had to keep pedaling. Every hill has a top. Just before hitting US 90, we crossed into Florida. Unfortunately, there was not a nice "Welcome to Florida" sign along this rural road, but we could identify the border by the change in highway quality. We lost our nice shoulder that Georgia had provided us. We were happy to be in a new state, our *first* state line crossing, but sad to leave behind the wonderful Georgia roads and courteous Georgia drivers.

We turned west onto US 90, and within a few miles we had entered the city of Chattahoochee, Florida. We decided to take our "Florida" picture at the welcome sign at the edge of town. Chattahoochee is home to the Florida State Hospital and is located at the south end of Lake Seminole. We decided that it was close to lunch time, and our options down the road looked limited, so we jogged a block off of our route to visit American Pie Pizza. The 15 inch Chicken Alfredo was delicious. Bob and I shared the pizza, but I am quite sure that I ate more than my allotted half. Sorry, Bob.

From Chattahoochee, US 90 continues west and descends down a long hill to cross the Apalachicola River. This was a nice hill, and although the wind chill on my face prevented me from pedaling up to a top speed, I still coasted down the long hill and hit 38 miles per hour! The Apalachicola River is also the time zone border, so we were back in the Central time zone. This was our **first** time zone crossing.

The river flows under a large bridge on US 90 and ends at the Gulf of Mexico. The Jim Woodruff Dam is just upstream from the bridge and can be seen in the distance from the highway bridge. I did not linger long on the bridge, since the north wind was blowing firm and steady. Now that we are on US 90 west of Chattahoochee, this is the **first** portion of our ride that is on the official Southern Tier bicycle route published by the Adventure Cycling Association.

From Chattahoochee, we followed US 90 west through Sneads and Grand Ridge. Both are very small communities that have been bypassed by Interstate 10. We did see a sign coming into Grand Ridge stating that it was the home of Miss Florida USA 2015; not bad for a town with a population of about 900. At Grand Ridge, we turned north (hello wind) for a mile and then west on county road 164A. This is the official southern tier route, and it took us off of US 90 for a time.

I have say "good job" to the ACA for this side route. Reddoch Road, or 164A, was a dream come true. The total distance on this road was 8 miles, and only 12 cars passed us in total (yes, I counted them). Both sides of the road had a nice shoulder, and the asphalt pavement was not very old. We were also able to see many Redbud trees in bloom, our **first** Redbud sighting. From Reddoch Road the route turned onto Blue Springs Road, and then Highway 71. This short stretch of highway did not have a shoulder, and the traffic was heavier. Soon, we were back on the familiar US 90 to enter Marianna, Florida.

We were happy to be entering our last town of the day, which would be our home for the night. We were not happy to see the narrow four lane through town, with no room for bicycles on the edge of the road. This was our **first** batch of rude motorists as well – sorry, Marianna residents, but I know you can do better. The law says to give bicycles at least 3 feet when passing, and several cars did not allow us that much room. One driver yelled and another honked at us. This seems to be odd behavior to me for a town than is on an established bicycle route, bringing untold thousands of out of state dollars to their community. We ended up on the sidewalks for most of our ride through town.

Soon the tension ended, and we arrived at the Executive Inn. The older (think 1960s) hotel was spartan, but fairly clean, and will be welcome accommodations for our tired bodies. It does have Wi-Fi, so all is not lost. The temperature was still a measly 46 degrees as we checked in. Tomorrow should be warmer.

A few reflections on the status of our bodies at this point in the journey. We are over 260 miles from the Atlantic Ocean, having ridden for five days now. My legs are sore in places, but not too fatigued. My neck and arms have strengthened and are no longer hurting. The real issue the last two days was my tushie. You know, my derriere, the back of my front, the fleshy part (so says Hawkeye in M*A*S*H). I believe it is toughening up because it was not as uncomfortable sitting on the seat today. Tomorrow should be about the same number of miles as today, but it will hopefully be warmer. That's all for now...

Apalachicola River south of Lake Seminole (time zone border).

Reddoch Road between Grand Junction and Marianna, FL.

Day 6: March 7, 2015 - Marianna to Mossy Head, FL - 71.8 miles

A Tough Day We Thought Would Be Easier

45 degrees to start, 78 degrees to finish, sunny, wind NE at 4 to 8 mph, 8:00 AM to 4:00 PM, 12.2 average mph, 28 mph max, 5:50 hours riding time.

The low last night was in the mid-30s, so we knew we would not be leaving before 8AM. The motel did not have breakfast, so we rode to McDonald's for breakfast and brought it back to the motel to eat and pack. We still managed to leave a few minutes after 8 AM.

While waiting on our food order, we chatted with three older gentlemen who had inquired about our trip. It was interesting that one of them was same age as Bob, 68. Bob suggested that he could get a bike and take a ride as well, to which local resident replied "why would I want a bike, I've got a Cadillac".

The morning was cold, but clear and sunny. We had put on many of our layers to keep us warm during the first few hours of the day. Today's route kept us on US 90, and there were not many towns to pass through on this section. Most of the route had a good shoulder for biking.

We also had the advantage of a slight tail wind for most of the day. The route took us out of Marianna and through the small communities of Cottondale, Chipley, Bonifay, Caryville, Westville, Ponce De Leon, Argyle, and Defuniak Springs. Defuniak Springs was the only town of any significant size.

For the first half of the day, the miles rolled by easily. We had a few climbs from time to time, but also many long, flat stretches where we could make good time. We had found a restaurant about 36 miles out, in Westville, called the Whistle Stop Cafe. We were really looking forward to a good lunch at this cafe with an intriguing name. However, even though it was the only restaurant in Westville, it had been closed down some time back and a For Rent sign was on the window. I believe this was the key to our day becoming tougher. We did find a gas station open that served barbeque sandwiches, so we purchased two for each of us. I think that was not enough lunch, because we started to run out of steam late in the afternoon. We took our sandwiches over to a park bench outside of the post office. We could actually see the closed restaurant where we had planned to eat, just over the railroad tracks. As I ate my lunch, enjoying the beautiful day, I told Bob that the only thing that would make it better would be if a train came through. Within five minutes, a train of flat cars with maintenance equipment came rolling down the tracks from east to west!

We pressed on to Defuniak Springs, a town of just over 5,000. According to the city website, the park in the middle of town includes one of the two perfectly round spring fed lakes in the world. The lake has a street around it with many historic buildings. While Bob tried to catch a short rest nap near the museum, I decided to ride around the lake and enjoy the old buildings and architecture.

Because we had arrived in Defuniak Springs at about 1 PM, we had a decision to make. Should we stay at the Adams Motel, which I am sure would be similar in quality to our motel last night, or should we ride another 16 miles to the next motel option? Since the weather was great and we had a slight tail wind, we decided to ride on.

I think our low food intake led to afternoon energy shortages. We took breaks every 5 or 6 miles, and we stopped at a store for Gatorade and snacks. These really helped, and we rode on to the motel, arriving around 4 PM. We were tired, but it felt good to ride the 72 miles today.

The ride today was primarily through all rural areas. We saw another pecan orchard, more stands of pine trees, and trees with Spanish moss. As I think about it, our route has been almost completely rural from the start. We have not had to ride through any big cities, and we have not yet seen any skyscrapers.

We did have an interesting dog encounter. We have been chased by a few dogs the last few days, but usually we can yell at them or just keep riding to stay ahead of them. Today, a large white dog was barking from the other side of a long fence. The dog was matching our speed, but we were not too worried because it was 30 yards away. The fence seemed like it would be good barrier. Well, when the dog reached the end of the yard, at a fence that separated the yard from the cemetery, the dog climbed the fence. From the open cemetery yard, it made a straight run for us. Luckily, we had gotten slightly ahead of it when it had to climb the fence. We put on a burst of speed and outran it after another 50 yards or so. Once I saw how fast Bob took off, I decided that he must have been holding back on me. I could see that he really could ride faster than he had been riding all morning!

The Econo Lodge is near the interstate, and the only two places to eat for several miles were a McDonald's and Subway. We decided that a couple of foot long sandwiches would hit the spot. We also passed the 300 mile mark today. I noticed it when we stopped for lunch, but we forgot to take a picture. We have ridden about 12% of the way across the country so far.

US 90 west of Marianna - good road surface and nice shoulder.

Lake Defuniak in Defuniak Springs - spring fed and nearly a perfect circle.

Day 7: March 8, 2015 - Mossy Head to Pensacola, FL - 62.0 miles

An Easier Day We Thought Would Be Tougher

50 degrees to start, 76 degrees to finish, sunny, wind SE at 5 to 10 mph, 9:30 AM to 5:00 PM, 12.0 average mph, 27 mph max, 5:10 hours riding time.

Yesterday was a tough day. It was long, but it was also a mentally tough day. You just have to push through those. We rode a long day and wound up in the middle of nowhere. The time change meant we would lose an hour, and the temptation would be to cut today short, or delay our start. Like one of the church signs we saw a few days back said: "Opportunity only knocks once, temptation knocks forever." We ate a light breakfast at the motel and rolled out about 9:30 AM. That gave us a little extra time, and also allowed the temperature to warm to about 50 degrees. Remember, that was really 8:30 AM before the time changed last night.

Speaking of yesterday, I really need to be writing down more of these experiences of riding a bike across the country with a 68 year old guy as my sidekick. Or maybe I am his sidekick. Anyway, it was during the first half of the day, and Bob saw something on the side of the road 50 yards in front of us. He calls back to me: "bicyclist ahead", and then in a few seconds he says "no, it is a mailbox". At this point, I yelled forward: "Bob, that's a pedestrian". And he tells me his glasses are fine... Our conversations are mostly yelled back and forth. Not so much due to Bob's poor hearing, of which it is, but mostly because we ride single file a lot of the time With road noise and wind noise it can be hard to hear what the other person is saying.

But, back to today... once we were out and riding, we started to feel much better. There is something therapeutic about the sun on your skin and the wind in your face and propelling yourself along under your own power. We had another slight tailwind today and it was wonderful. These bikes run so smoothly and amaze me. At one point today, we got a good gust of wind from behind and it felt like the bike could just lift off of the ground. It did not, by the way.

After only 14 miles, we entered Crestview, Florida. We had intended to eat something here, since the free motel breakfast was minimal. We stopped at the local Pic N Save (grocery store) and grabbed four bananas and two bottles of sports drink. We intended to prevent the energy issues that we had encountered yesterday. There are not many towns between Crestview and Milton, two towns with 20,000 and 9,000 people. We are using the Southern Tier map at this point, and it indicated some kind of cafe in Holt, so we planned to stop at Holt for lunch.

Somewhere around Milligan, we passed a young man, maybe 35, pushing a baby stroller with a large camo backpack in it. We waved and said hello, but it would been interesting to stop and hear his story. He appeared to be going quite a distance.

Most of the landscape today has been open fields and small pine tree forests. The railroad line has kept us company much of the day, but it was interesting that only one train passed us.

We arrived at the tiny community of Holt, Florida, just after noon. There was a small diner, aptly named Holts Diner, on the north side of the road, and we have learned to take the first option that presents itself. It may be the only option. The diner was nearly empty, so we sat next to the window that overlooked our bikes. We do lock them with a small cable and padlock, although that mostly is just for peace of mind.

I ordered the blue plate special #1: chicken fried steak with white gravy on a bed of rice, with green beans and bacon, coleslaw, fried okra, a dinner roll, and a sweet tea. D-lish. It was excellent. It was a hearty meal that was as close to home cooked as we will get out here on the road. I ate every morsel and felt rejuvenated. A good, solid meal really makes a significant difference when riding these kinds of miles.

We had been riding US 90 all day, and we would essentially stay on US 90 for the rest of the day. It has been a good road to us - nice shoulder, light traffic, and a smooth surface. According to the official Southern Tier route, we were supposed to divert off of US 90 and take back roads to Milton. However, a quick look with Google's satellite view last night told me that those roads did not look very good. That route would also be about 7 miles longer than staying on US 90. We did not have any complaints with our old friend US 90, so we stayed with her all the way to Milton.

There was an interesting point of interest (wait, I think that is redundant) that we saw along our route. We would have completely missed this if we had stayed on the Southern Tier official route. Somewhere parallel to US 90 east of Milton, we encountered a brick road with the following sign: Historical Florida State Route 1, Old Brick Road, Opened in 1921. It had apparently been preserved for a walking or bike trail. We moved over and rode this old remnant for a mile or so. It was inspiring to see how well much of the brick surface had survived. However, it was not nearly as smooth as the asphalt shoulder on US 90, so we left nostalgia behind and switched back to the modern replacement.

We soon approached Milton, and this would be the start of more urban areas all the way to Pensacola. On the east side of Milton, our route crossed the Blackwater River. There was some construction on the bridges over this waterway, and one of them had a metal grate road surface. This required steady hands and careful concentration, since the tires did not seem to grip as well on these metal grates. After this bridge, we were ready for a break anyway, and we spied a small river front park on the north side of the road. We took a side street and wound up at Riverwalk Park in Milton. This was a nice rest stop to eat a banana, protein bar, and rest our legs.

From Milton, we continued our westward journey, now with four lanes of traffic but still a good shoulder. The tailwind was strong again, and we rode many miles at 15 to 18 mph. It felt great. We were back on the official Southern Tier route again.

We were soon riding through Pace, a city of 20,000 on the northeast side of Escambia Bay. We knew by looking at the maps that a large bridge was likely just ahead between Pace and Pensacola. Another rest break would be helpful, so we stopped at a Burger King for a tropical mango smoothie. That was very refreshing.

Knowing that our hotel for the night was not far away, we started riding again with good energy. We had to cross another long bridge with a metal grate road surface, which was also in another construction area. The cars gave us good space for the most part. I am certainly glad that we are highly visible mostly because of our red flashing rear LED lights. The last bridge was a long, high, arching bridge at the north side of Escambia Bay. Traffic was heavier, but the bridge had a wide concrete shoulder. This was appreciated.

Not long after we left the west end of the bridge, our route turned south to follow Scenic Highway 90 along the edge of the bay. The traffic was considerably lighter now, and the gently rolling hills provided a short climb every now and then. This stretch of the route passed many large, nice homes that overlook the bay. It also had a very unusual house with gold roofs and many yard ornaments - you would have to see it to appreciate it. It was a nice section to ride for sure.

Right after Scenic Highway 90 crossed over I-10 (with a nice view of the I-10 bridge over the bay), we found that our hotel was there on our route. This turned out to be a great location for us and a good place to end our day. The hotel, a Quality Inn, has been renovated and is on the level with many Hyatt properties that I have stayed in. It will also provide a nice breakfast in the morning.

One problem each evening is that we need to eat dinner, but do not have a car to drive to a restaurant. Many times, we do not want to ride another several miles to eat either. As luck would have it tonight, there was a Dairy Queen right across the street from our hotel. Not only that, it had large glass windows in the dining area that overlooked Escambia Bay and the I-10 and railroad bridges. I splurged and had my first soda of the trip tonight at dinner.

The day was not easy, but it was certainly easier than we were expecting this morning. The winds were with us, and the ride was very enjoyable. We took a few more breaks and ate better today. We feel really good at the end of our first week. If the rain does not keep us in tomorrow, this may be our last night in Florida. We should also pass the 400 mile mark tomorrow. Good night to all.

Brick road FL SR 1 from 1921 alongside our old friend, US 90, east of Milton.

Riverwalk Park in Milton, FL - A nice place for a rest break.

Alabama

Day 8: March 9, 2015 - Pensacola, FL to Dauphin Island, AL - 67.9 miles

A Brief Rain Shower then an Amazing Tailwind

60 degrees to start, 75 degrees to finish, sunny, wind E at 10 to 15 mph, 8:00 AM to 5:00 PM, 13.2 average mph, 33 mph max, 5:05 hours riding time.

We knew that today had a significant chance of rain, so our fail safe plan would be to make 35 miles or so to Orange Beach if we had to ride in much rain. We had a very good breakfast at the Quality Inn, and we were back on Scenic Highway 90 just after 8 AM this morning. It was cloudy, so we had our rain jackets in the top of our panniers. Sure enough, about 2 miles down the road the rain started to fall. It was a light steady shower, not a downpour. We found a nice large tree at one of the residence driveways, so we pulled off to add our rain layer. We also had to be extra careful on the slick pavement.

Our first stop this morning, about 9 miles in, was at Bikes Plus on North Palafox Street in Pensacola. The folks there were very helpful and got right to work on Bob's bike. He was having problems getting into his lowest gear, which was needed on the steepest hills. They made the necessary adjustments and also fixed a brake cable that looked suspect. We really appreciated their fast and quick service. Our entire stop took about an hour or so, and then we were back on the road. The rain had stopped, and we were able to wind our way out of Pensacola on drying pavement.

We were on the official Southern Tier route again today. We stayed close to the Gulf coast all day, passing the Pensacola Naval Air Station entrance and Big Lagoon State Park on the Gulf Beach Highway. We had to cross a large bridge over to Perdido Key, and that east wind was really blowing as a crosswind since the bridge ran north and south.

At the very top of the bridge, I stopped briefly to let Bob catch up, and another cyclist going the other direction crossed over to our side to chat. Her name was Dot, and she and Hannah had started in San Diego in January. Dot took a bad fall during a dog encounter, broke her collarbone, and had been forced to ride a moped for the last 4 weeks. Her friend Hannah took the moped today, and it was Dot's first day back on the bike. This was our first meeting with west to east riders.

After a nice run down the other side of the bridge, we turned back to the west. The tailwind today was amazing. We were running 15 to 18 mph for miles at a time. Other than having to climb over a few bridges, the ride today was very flat indeed. We crossed from Florida to Alabama before lunch and were soon pedaling past Orange Beach. This had been our short ride option, but we decided to take full advantage of the wind today.

Not far into Alabama, we stopped for lunch at Rotolo's Pizzeria. I had the muffuletta small pizza and it was very good. If you have never had it as a sandwich or otherwise, it contains pepperoni, Canadian bacon, salami, and Italian olive salad. While we ate lunch, we looked ahead out our options and distances. We decided that with the amazing tailwind, we could easily make the last ferry from Fort Morgan to Dauphin Island.

As always, a lunch stop provided renewed energy. We continued riding out Perdido Beach Boulevard, which had great bike lanes. In fact, all of today had good bike lanes or shoulders. We made a detour through Gulf State Park, and continued out highway 180 towards the end of the peninsula. At many times, we were easily moving at 18 to 21 mph. The wind was our best friend today.

We noticed the peninsula getter narrower and narrower as we headed west. Soon, we rolled by the Fort Morgan Historic Site. This fort was completed around 1833 to protect Mobile Bay. This would have been quite an accomplishment for an engineer in those days. Its partner, Fort Gaines, is located on Dauphin Island.

We made our way to the front of the queue for the ferry, and we had made such good time that we would be able to take the 4:15 ferry across to Dauphin Island. We were very excited. While waiting for the ferry, we met two other bicyclists. Zora and Ellena had finished college not too long ago and were bicycling together from Savannah to New Orleans. These friends were camping along the way, and they had also carried their musical instruments - a mandolin and a clarinet. We had a nice chat on the ferry ride, and I am sure it made Bob's day. He always enjoys meeting someone new.

The ferry ride was about 3 or 4 miles across the entrance to Mobile Bay, and it was only $5.00 for cyclists. It is a small ferry that is open, with no cabin for passengers, and only holds about 18 cars. We soon landed at Dauphin Island, and headed toward the motel near the west end.

After checking in at the Gulf Breeze motel and getting back on the bikes for a one mile ride to a restaurant (not much is open on Mondays this time of year), we are now back in our room resting and writing. We feel very fortunate to have made such good progress today and to have avoided much of the rain.

Incidentally, if you have not found Bob's blog (Robert Reynolds) on CrazyGuyOnABike.com, you can find it here:

http://www.crazyguyonabike.com/doc/Zoot2015

Also, we have been playing a little game with some of the readers back home. We have been using a mystery word of the day in each day's journal. Both Bob and I will use a new mystery word each day. Jana has guessed almost every one of them correctly. We randomly generate a new word for each day, and then have to find a way to use it in our journals. If you are interested, the words for previous days are: Day 1 = smoke, day 2 = immigrant, day 3 = advertise, day 4 = pocket watch, day 5 = snail, day 6 = skyscraper, day 7 = skin, day 8 = ???

We are doing well. Today was a success mentally as well as geographically. After 8 days we have now bicycled across Georgia, Florida, and into Alabama. Our total miles ridden stands at 463 miles.

Bridge across to Perdido Key, Florida - Highway 292.

We crossed into our third state today – Alabama.

Mississippi

Day 9: March 10, 2015 - Dauphin Island, AL to Gautier, MS - 48.3 miles

Another Forecast of Rain that Wasn't

70 degrees to start, 78 degrees to finish, cloudy, then foggy, then partly cloudy, then sunny, wind SE at 5 to 10 mph, 9:00 AM to 2:30 PM, 11.9 average mph, 34 mph max, 4:00 hours riding time. The random mystery word for yesterday used by Bob and me was: engineer.

Verse of the Day: "...with men this is impossible, but with God all things are possible." Matthew 19:26

The Gulf Breeze Motel on Dauphin Island ended up being a fine place to stay, but it did not have breakfast. So, we rolled out around 8:30 AM in search of breakfast somewhere on the island. Actually, we had already located and read rave reviews of a fantastic bakery near the entrance to the island. We rode the short distance to the Lighthouse Bakery, mouths watering, stomachs growling, and then spirits falling as we saw the sign in the front window: Closed Tuesdays. We ended up with a Subway breakfast sandwich, so we still managed to get in our protein. However, a heavenly cinnamon roll would have been so nice. Oh well...

The fog was rolling in as we left the motel, but by the time we finished breakfast, the sun had come out and the fog was started to dissipate. As we left Subway, we chatted briefly with someone outside. He commented that "it was not a very good day for a bike ride." I disagreed, but kept it to myself. The temperature was perfect, the wind was again at our back for the most part, and the fog was lifting. The rain also looked to be holding off for the time being. We had not yet decided on a destination for the day, since the rain chances were so high.

To get from Dauphin Island back to the mainland, you head north on Highway 193. You essentially cross a 3.5 mile long bridge with a large arch in the middle that is 85 feet in the air. It rained off and on all night, so the roads were very wet. The road surface was good, and the shoulder was wide, so we rolled along on the bridge at a good pace. The arch in the middle looked very high, but as we got closer and started climbing, it did not seem so bad. Traffic was also light this morning, so that was helpful to us. I love climbing these bridges. I really do. They are not difficult if you down shift and keep your feet spinning. You may slow down to 5 miles per hour, but persistence will pay off. That payoff is the run down the other side. The problem this morning was that I had to ride the brakes and keep the bike under 35 mph to be safe on the wet pavement. It was still a lot of fun.

We were still on the official Southern Tier route, riding north on highway 193, and then turning west on highway 188 at Alabama Port. The shoulders were good and drivers were courteous. After about 10 miles or so the pavement had even dried under our wheels. Following 188, we went through the communities of Coden and Bayou La Batre. We crossed our first drawbridge on the trip at Bayou La Batre. It was a nice point of interest that was apparently constructed in 1984. As we were leaving that small town, we stopped at a fruit stand on the side of the road. They had bananas and other fruit for sale, so we purchased four bananas. They are excellent snacks in the morning and afternoons. We ate one there, and then packed away the other for later. The last memorable facet of the town was the very large, old trees near the highway at some of the homes. I believe they were live oaks, but I was too busy watching traffic to be sure.

We continued our ride on highway 188 and arrived at Grand Bay, Alabama, just before noon. This seemed like a good lunch stop, so we rode towards the interstate and found a local eatery - Sam's Super Burger. I had the 'new' fish sandwich and a peanut butter hand spun milkshake. They were very both quite delicious. This was a nice stop for us, and the lunch and rest break were energizing.

At this point, we had a decision to make. Actually, we had already made a decision, but I will describe our thought process. The official Southern Tier route from Grand Bay travels north, and then winds on many back roads. Sometimes the official road name and the name on a sign, or lack of a sign, differ and make those roads difficult to follow. We would also be out of touch with places to eat or stay for over 100 miles. We decided to deviate from the official route and take US 90 west at Grand Bay. US 90 had been good to us back in Florida and Alabama, so we were hopeful that it would carry us safely towards Gulfport, Mississippi. That would be our new turn northward. We planned to take state route 53 to Bogalusa, Louisiana. We could then pick up the official Southern Tier route at that city if we wanted.

We turned west again and rode US 90 out of Grand Bay, Alabama. The shoulders continued to be nice, wide and smooth. This abruptly changed at the Mississippi state line. It was exciting to enter a new state, our fourth on the trip, but we lost the shoulder completely at the state line. Within a mile though, the highway divided, went to four lanes, and added a shoulder. This was much appreciated. However, the shoulder was not the fine specimen that we had learned to love on US 90 back in Alabama and Florida. This Mississippi shoulder was old and rugged.

It had been neglected and left for dead. We tolerated the rough ride for a while, but then large cracks appeared from which were growing hardy weeds and tough grasses. Every four feet was a harsh bump in the road through the vegetation. We ended up riding the white line of the right lane, watching our rear view mirrors for approaching cars, and then moving into the shoulder if the cars did not move to the left lane to pass us. This maneuver was sometimes done with tight grips and gritted teeth. It actually was not that scary.

After about 5 miles of this torture, the road surface changed, including the shoulder. We were back on smooth material and ecstatic to be there. Traffic was increasing as we approached Pascagoula, Mississippi, but the shoulder was wide and in good condition. We did divert off of US 90 onto a frontage road through the town. This moved us away from some of the traffic and allowed us to bypass a few of the traffic lights.

Late in the afternoon, we pulled into a Walgreen's for Gatorade, toothpaste, and aspirin. Too much detail? As we were back outside of the store loading things onto our bikes, a lady approached us and asked where we were headed. I told her "ultimately, to San Diego", and she said that she used to live in San Diego near Ocean Beach. I replied that we were actually going to end our ride at Ocean Beach. She gave a few words of encouragement as we departed the sidewalk.

Between Pascagoula and Gautier we crossed another tall, long bridge. This was another long climb with the usual task of debris-dodging while on the bridge shoulder. By and large, the shoulder on highways contains a lot of road debris. It gets bounced off the road by traffic, but if it lands on the shoulder, it is usually there to stay. On bridges with a concrete barrier, debris that may have been thrown off into the grass is reflected back onto the shoulder. Nothing can escape it. We have seen glass bottles, broken mirrors, shoes, beads, scissors, bolts, nuts, assorted hardware, wood, nails, a knife, rocks, gravel, sand, gloves, pieces of tires, a box of sweetener packets, dead animals, etc. You have to be very careful to watch for items that might cause a flat tire. You have to be especially careful when flying down the other side of a bridge at 30 mph. This brings me back to the last bridge I was climbing today. The best case scenario is when you look in your rear view mirror and see that it is "clear back". At that point, I shifted over into the traffic lane (no debris there), pump the pedals for several seconds, tuck in, and enjoy the ride. Today's bridges were running between 30 and 35 mph, but these bicycles are smooth as silk. Don't try this at home kids, we are professionals.

The highway and the winds lined back up nicely for the last several miles, so we sailed along at a good clip into Gautier, Mississippi. The motel reviews were mixed, but the Magnolia Inn must have done some updating. The place is quite nice. It is a little pricier than I think it should be, but there are only about two choices in Gautier. Supply and demand in action.

We rode a short day today at only 48 miles. This will give us more time in the afternoon to rest and recover. The forecast is calling for high chances of rain for the next several days, so that may cause us to adjust our plans. I am very thankful to the Lord for the great weather we have had so far. I know the rain falls on the just and the unjust alike, but the weather and the experience have definitely been a blessing so far.

I think I might insert another interesting 'Bob' anecdote at this point. When we stop for a rest break, often on the side of the road, he always takes off his gloves and helmet. That is not unusual, but nearly every time we stop, he will throw his gloves and helmet on the ground. I keep saying, "Bob, if you will lay those on your panniers (saddle bags), you won't have to pick them up". His response is always, "I know". But then, when our break is over, he grunts and groans when he leans over to pick up those gloves and helmet. Funny stuff.

The rain delayed our trip out for dinner. We found a place within walking distance, less than 1/2 mile. It looks like we caught a gap in the rain and are now back, still dry. Dustin gave me a hard time today, telling me that we were supposed to be camping and cooking noodles. I had told my friend Dustin before we left that we intended to camp and cook out most of the days on our trip. We are definitely equipped to do that, but I will blame it on Bob. The motels are much better for him to get much needed rest.

Well, another day done, and over 500 miles on this grand adventure. Still no flat tires. We will see how tomorrow goes with the predicted rain. So far, so good. Oh, and the rain just started up again.

Bridge from Dauphin Island back to the mainland. It is 3.5 miles long with a large hump in the middle, about 85 feet high.

Large trees lining a driveway on the outskirts of Bayou La Batre, MS. Very nice.

Day 10: March 11, 2015 - Gautier to Gulfport, MS - 32.4 miles

Another Shorter Day, Staging for Tomorrow

66 degrees to start, 72 degrees to finish, cloudy, 9:00 AM to 12:30 PM, 11.8 average mph, 24 mph max, 2:45 hours riding time. The random mystery word for yesterday used by Bob and me was: knife.

Verse of the Day: "I am able to do all things through Christ who strengthens me..." Philippians 4:13. This is the verse at the bottom of my information cards that we hand out to those who ask if we are blogging or journaling the trip.

Yesterday and today were partial rest days to allow us to recover and strengthen. There was a good chance of rain this afternoon, so we rode during the morning to try to avoid the rain for one last day. This was also a staging day, logistically. We are now in Gulfport, Mississippi. From here, we ride northeast to Bogalusa, Louisiana. The ride will be about 65 miles, but there are no other towns or services on the route. Thus our stop in north Gulfport to ready ourselves for tomorrow, and it puts us as close to Louisiana as possible.

I was fairly impressed with the room at the Magnolia Inn last night, but breakfast this morning completely blew their rating. We had been trying to find lower cost places to stay that offered Wi-Fi and a free breakfast. Most of the breakfasts have been sufficient, with some obviously better than others. Today, our options were cereal with warm, watery milk and English muffins. Yes folks that was it. I went ahead and ate a few bowls of cereal and had a toasted piece of bread. We have to eat, you know. I will say that the room was very clean and the staff were friendly. As we checked out this morning, she said, "Where are ya'll going again?" I told her our destination, and here response was "That's awesome. Crazy, but awesome."

Since today would be a shorter distance day, we allowed ourselves a little extra time this morning to be more leisurely as we packed to depart. We rolled out onto the shoulder of US 90 heading west again just after 9:00 AM. This highway is getting more congested along the Gulf coast as towns are more frequent. I tried a new method for today's route. I have used Google Maps with the bicycle routing option before, but often I modify it after I see their suggestion. Today, we basically followed Google's route almost exactly. The aspect of today's route that I liked was the fact that Google moved us off of US 90 after about 10 miles onto secondary roads in the towns along the way. This allowed us to deal with less traffic in some areas.

As we entered Ocean Springs, Mississippi, we rode on streets through town on the south side of US 90. There were many boutiques, specialty stores, and other interesting retail establishments on the west end of Ocean Springs. We also passed the entrance to Gulf Islands National Seashore. The best reason for being on the south side of US 90 was that it allowed easy access to the bicycle and pedestrian lane on the Biloxi Bay Bridge. The old bridge was destroyed by Hurricane Katrina. The new bridge was designed to provide for six lanes of traffic with an additional, protected, ten foot bike and pedestrian lane on the south side of the bridge. The view of Biloxi Bay is fantastic, since the new bridge is approximately 100 feet above the bay below. Our view of Biloxi Bay would also be the last body of saltwater that we will see until San Diego.

As we exited the bridge on the west end, we entered the city of Biloxi. We turned north, crossed US 90, and rode the back roads through Biloxi and Gulfport. If you are a cyclist looking to follow this route, the main streets we travelled were Magnolia, Mill, Washington, Howard, Irish Hill, Pass, and Airport Road.

Points of interest along this route included Keesler Air Force Base, some nice old homes near Brickyard Bayou, bike storage pods at the Biloxi terminal of the Coast Transit Authority (CTA), and Gulfport-Biloxi International Airport.

We found an IHOP not far from our motel in north Gulfport, and we stopped in for our second breakfast and lunch. The omelet and pancakes were delicious. As we were leaving the restaurant, an older gentleman stopped us and asked if we were runners. We explained that we were bicyclists headed to San Diego. We chatted for a few minutes and learned that John had retired from the Navy and then worked in a shipyard until he retired again. At one point, he asked if we were going to counseling to help deal with our insanity! He was kidding, of course. At least I think he was. He was very nice, and said, "God bless you guys" a few times before we parted. Thank you for your service and your encouragement, John.

We have again managed to miss the rain. It does appear to be headed this way tonight. Rain chances are 80% tomorrow and 100% Friday. Tomorrow may be a long, wet ride, so we will be resting up tonight after this shorter day of biking. We hope to leave before 8 AM. At least it is not supposed to be cold.

After 10 days on the road, I am starting to feel like an exile since I have been away from home for so long. We have 544 miles behind us, and we should push beyond the 600 mile mark tomorrow. Today's journal entry was short, but thanks for reading.

View of Ocean Springs Beach from the US 90 bridge over Biloxi Bay in Mississippi. You can also see Bob pedaling up the bike lane on the left side of the photo.

Bicycle storage pods to protect bikes from the elements at the Biloxi CTA terminal. Very cool.

Louisiana

Day 11: March 12, 2015 - Gulfport, MS to Bogalusa, LA - 68.4 miles

Meeting a New Friend from London in State #5

67 degrees to start, 72 degrees to finish, cloudy and rainy, 7:30 AM to 4:00 PM, wind SE at 4 to 8 mph, 11.8 average mph, 27 mph max, 5:45 hours riding time. The random mystery word for yesterday was: exile.

Verse of the Day: "(if) My people who are called by My name humble themselves, pray and seek My face, and turn from their evil ways, then I will hear from heaven, forgive their sin, and heal their land" - 2 Chronicles 7:14. I saw many yard signs in Georgia with this verse reference.

Well, we finally got rained on today, but it was not as bad as we were expecting. We awoke early, about 6:30 AM this morning, and headed down to the motel's breakfast area. The breakfast was surprisingly complete for a motel costing less than $60 (America's Best Value). We enjoyed sausage, biscuits and gravy, eggs, cereal, juice, and coffee. This would be good fuel for our engine today. We rolled out of the parking lot about 7:30 AM, after sunrise, but the sun was nowhere to be seen. It was a drizzly, cloudy, gloomy day.

We crossed US 49 and headed north to leave Gulfport. It was a hectic first couple of miles, since US 49 is about 12 lanes of traffic, and we had to pass under Interstate 10 as well. At one of the stoplights, a lady came up beside us with her window rolled down as she started to turn right. I looked over, and she said, "You all be careful, we will be praying for you." I said that we appreciated that, and off she went. That chance encounter was a boost to our morning.

From US 49 we planned to jog west off of the busy highway and run north on a parallel road. It was clear that we would have to have a death wish to attempt to move to the left turn lanes. So, like in Disney's *Cars* movie, we decided to turn right to go left. We turned right at the light, made a U turn in the road, and then could cross with the light to ultimately be going west or left. Follow that?

We wound our way on a few back roads before intersecting Highway 53. We continued northwest on highway 53 towards Poplarville. The roads were rural, passing many farms and ranches. We have started to see a few green fields with cattle. The road did not have a shoulder, but drivers were again very courteous and gave us plenty of room. It rained on us lightly, but only an easy shower for an hour or two. We put on our rain jackets for the first few miles, but after a short rest stop, we left the jackets off and rode in the rain. It was too warm for the jackets to be comfortable.

I did pass the time for about 25 miles by having Bob help me memorize "A Psalm of Life" by Longfellow. I managed to memorize it all, but will have to review it the next several days to cement it in memory. It ends like this: *Let us then be up and doing, with a heart for any fate, still achieving, still pursuing, learn to labor and to wait.*

We arrived in Poplarville just after noon, and we planned to grab some lunch there before turning west on Highway 26. We made it to the one stoplight in town, and had to stop and wait for the light to change. Just as it turned green and we started to roll, we heard someone from behind us call out, "Hey, wait, wait!". We turned to look behind us and were surprised to see another bicycle tourer. We all pulled our bikes onto the median at the intersection and began to chat. We met a new friend, Will, who is from London. He and a friend had taken their bikes from England to South America. They had bicycled over 16,000 miles in the last 22 months, riding through Brazil, Argentina, Colombia, Mexico, and many other countries in South and Central America. They then rode into Texas and were heading east, with a final destination of New York. It was astounding to meet another cyclist on a long tour who was from London in this small Mississippi town. It is about the size of Tishomingo, Oklahoma – perhaps 3,000 residents. It seems that Will has already written up his impressions of us, and you can read what he thought here: http://www.contoursofacountry.com/encounters/usa/

After we exchanged cards and said goodbye, we continued on to Hardees for lunch. We needed to have something quick to try to stay ahead of the rain. The rain had stopped an hour or so before lunch, and we were actually just about dried out with the wind blowing over us as we rode. A gentleman two booths away asked where we were headed. We explained our story, and he asked several more questions, seeming quite interested. He also wished us luck as he left.

Somewhere on Highway 26 west of Poplarville, Mississippi, I reached over to my right side bar end shifter, and it came loose in my hand! I had noticed it slightly loose, but it had now come out of the handlebar end. I held it in place with my right hand in order to not lose any parts. I essentially was reduced to three gears, being able to only move the front derailleur between the three front cogs. I limped along for a mile or two, since there was not a shoulder on which to stop. We came to a bridge, and I was able to pull over onto the concrete shoulder just after crossing the bridge. It was now time to put my engineering skills and tool kit to good use, since there was not a nearby REI to try to take them up on any guarantee. I had wondered how those shifters were attached, and it was now time to find out. I removed the shift lever, found the disconnected screw and wedge clamp mechanism, and put it all back together. In about 15 minutes we were back on the road, and I was happy that it was an easy repair.

We soon left Mississippi and rolled into our fifth state - Louisiana. We also crossed over the Pearl River, which was about two feet above flood stage with all of the rain that this area has received lately.

We were soon in Bogalusa, Louisiana. An early industry in the town was a large sawmill, which for many years in the early 1900s was the largest in the world. The sawmill is gone, but a paper mill remains in operation today. The population is just over 12,000 people. We rode into town to check out the Budget Inn, the only motel close to our route in Bogalusa. It looked pretty shabby, and we could not find anyone in the office. So, we called a couple of other places, and decided to ride down to the Traveler's Rest. It was two miles south of our route, but they had Wi-Fi and ESPN. We were hoping to watch the OU-OSU basketball game tonight!

I let Bob have the shower first, and I rode back into town for a few supplies and dinner. I had my first mishap turning into the Walgreen's parking lot. Their curb into the drive had a 3 inch lip, and then angled up to the parking lot. This lack of a smooth transition, combined with the wet pavement from a recent rain shower, resulted in my bike sprawled out on the drive and my body doing some interesting dance moves to keep from being hurt. My gloves took the brunt of it, and no permanent damage was done.

I stopped by Taco Bell for some dinner, and I am sure that Ron's boys would be proud. They love Taco Bell. While I was waiting on the order, the lady running the register asked me how far I was riding. I told her that I was riding to California. She said to me, "Oh, really. Well, how far have you gone so far?" I told her that we had ridden about 600 miles from the Atlantic Ocean. Her response was "What?! Are you serious?" We certainly experience some humorous reactions from time to time.

Well, overall it was a good day. We rode some long miles, but did not get drenched. A few dogs made a run at us, but none were too dangerous. We logged a new state, and we are ready to watch OU play basketball. We also rolled past the 600 mile mark on our journey, and we were thrilled to chat with Will from London.

Rural highway 53 between Gulfport and Poplarville, MS. Nice road, nice drivers, even with the lack of a shoulder.

We met Will today in Poplarville, MS, of all places. He and a friend have ridden 16,000 miles through South and Central America. It was a nice visit.

Day 12: March 13, 2015 - Bogalusa to Amite, LA - 49.1 miles

The Day the Rain Would Not End

65 degrees to start, 70 degrees to finish, cloudy and rainy, 9:30 AM to 3:30 PM, wind SW at 5 to 10 mph, 10.8 average mph, 27 mph max, 4:30 hours riding time. The random mystery word for yesterday used by Bob and me was: guarantee.

The forecast for today was rain until noon, then ending. Because of this forecast, we decided to leave a bit later this morning, hoping for a nicer afternoon. As we left the motel, it was raining moderately. A lady waiting under the eave said that we were going to get wet. I told her maybe so. Her response was "there ain't no maybe about it" - it made me smile.

We rolled out to the street in front of the motel, and were taken aback by the large tidal waves of water that the passing cars were sending in our direction. We rode back to the center of Bogalusa to find some breakfast, and our rain jackets kept us mostly dry up to that point. After breakfast, we headed west on highway 10. It was a steady rain and 65 degrees, but our churning legs were keeping us warm. After about 24 miles and a few brief breaks, we were entering Franklinton, Louisiana.

Franklinton is a small town of less than 4,000. We rode into town looking for somewhere to eat lunch. We found a local cafe and started to park our bikes outside on the sidewalk. One of the local patrons came out and began to chat. We told him that drivers had been very friendly this morning. He responded that it could be due to the fact that a local judge is also a cyclist. This judge was passed too closely by a vehicle, but the judge was able to remember his license plate and called him up after the incident. Thanks, judge. The gentleman went on to describe where he lived on the edge of town and that he would be happy to put us up for the night in his pool house. He thought the pool was still too cold to swim in though. That was a nice gesture by a local resident that lived on Holiday Road. We failed to get his name.

After a tasty lunch, the Friday special at the Fair City Cafe, we headed back out. It was after noon, and the rain had stopped. Before long however, the rain showers started again. We did notice Holiday Road outside of town, and I appreciated the man's offer from earlier. We continued to ride highway 16 in the rain for a couple more hours after lunch. I did not mind the rain so much. It was not too cold, the shoulder was very wide today, and drivers were giving us plenty of room. The main complaint is that with the rain hitting me in the face and speckling my glasses, I am not able to look around as much and enjoy the passing countryside.

Later in the afternoon, the rain stopped and the clouds even broke to reveal the sun. We quickly had to pull to the side of the road and remove our rain gear. The sun was steaming us in our jackets! It was nice to now ride under partly cloudy skies. But this was short lived, and in a few more miles we were once again being rained on. This time, we just kept pedaling and left our rain gear in the panniers. We were within five or so miles of the destination hotel.

We were soon rolling into the edge of Amite, Louisiana. The city of Amite is pronounced AY-MEET, according to the hotel desk clerk. This small town is on an interstate, and the population is just over 4,000 residents. One big event is an Oyster festival each year in late March, but we are about a week too early. It is reported to have carnival games and musical entertainment, although likely not an orchestra.

It was one of those days that you have to just push through. The rain slowed us down, and the landscape did not have many notable features. The Arkel Dry Lites did keep all of our gear dry, and we were happy about that. Tomorrow looks to be nice and dry. Our goal is to reach New Roads and take a day or two rest.

Highway 16 west of Franklinton, during a break in the rain.

Old train station in Amite, LA, that has apparently been repurposed as the police station. That's recycling!

Day 13: March 14, 2015 - Amite to New Roads, LA - 70 miles

We Have Crossed the Mississippi

65 degrees to start, 74 degrees to finish, cloudy then partly sunny, 8:30 AM to 5:30 PM, 10.1 average mph, 27 mph max, 6:50 hours riding time. The random mystery word for yesterday was: orchestra.

Verse of the Day: "Repent and be baptized, each of you, in the name of Jesus Christ for the forgiveness of your sins, and you will receive the gift of the Holy Spirit" - Acts 2:38. I saw this one on a large billboard a day or so back.

Some days are easier to start than others, but today was a tough day to start. Much of the battle in this journey has been mental. Our legs are holding up well, but sometimes your mind wants to tell you that it is too difficult. This morning, we put one of Newton's laws into action, and things improved from there. Once a body is in motion, it tends to stay in motion.

We had a hot, solid breakfast at the hotel, and good fuel for our engine is always beneficial. Another uplifting item was a message from the kind folks at the Waffle House in Thomasville, Georgia. I remember we chatted with Lois there some days back. They had emailed a note of encouragement this morning, and we really appreciated it.

We were off of our planned route again today, trying to ride west from Amite to New Roads. I had built a new route and had all of the distances and turns written on a piece of paper. The smaller rural roads were not marked on our state map. It was a nice ride today on these back roads. We had wonderful views of farms and fields and wooded lanes. Courteous drivers were again plentiful on our route today.

Our morning was cloudy and looked like rain, but the rain never came. It was cool enough that I added my sleeves. It was one of those dreary days, at least to start, when you would look forward to a steamy bowl of stew for lunch. But the weather would not be dreary all day. For all but an hour stretch of rough, bumpy pavement, we had good roads or shoulders. We would make a turn, calculate in our head what the odometer should be for the next turn, and then watch for that new road or highway.

We knew that we might not find any services on our back road route, so we were loaded with protein bars, trail mix, and bananas for regular snacks. Sometime before Slaughter, the clouds began to break and the sun started to come out. Before long, we were surrounded by an energizing, uplifting warmth. The sun always seems to improve our day and our spirits.

At Slaughter, we detoured by a local gas station to see what warm food options they might have. From the signs on the wall and the interior appearance, this establishment had been around for some time. They had cheeseburgers, even at 2PM when we came by, and it was actually quite tasty. We took a short break here to regain some strength and sit on a larger seat.

Back on the road, we continued our meandering navigation. We enjoyed shaded lanes where in many places the trees completely covered the road. Finally, we made it to US Highway 61, shortly before turning on LA 10. We made a pit stop at a gas station, although making it across the busy four lane was somewhat challenging. While outside on the sidewalk, a lady walked by and asked if I was here for the big bike race. I asked her about the race. She explained that there was a 140 mile race tomorrow, starting in St. Francisville. I told her that we were riding cross country and would not be in that race, but planned to spend the night in New Roads. She then recommended that we eat at Hot Tails for dinner and wished us well.

We were soon making a turn onto Louisiana Highway 10, and within a few miles we approached the John James Audubon Bridge. Up until 2011, crossing the Mississippi River in this area was done via a ferry to St. Francisville. The ferry had to be closed, and bicyclists and motorists now use this new cable-stayed bridge. The bridge is a beautiful bit of engineering, and it is also the second longest cable-stayed bridge in the Western Hemisphere with a total length of over 2 miles.

We stopped at many places on the shoulder to enjoy the view and take photos. The bridge has a good shoulder for cyclists, and now that we are back on the official Southern Tier route, I am sure that the bridge serves quite a number of them annually. Crossing the Mississippi River is a significant milestone for us. We have ridden over 700 miles, and crossing the Mississippi was an encouraging accomplishment. Many weeks ago, as I sat at the dining room table reviewing maps, New Roads seemed light years away.

On the way down the west end of the bridge, Bob and I separated. This often happens down hills or down long bridge descents. The head wind kept my speed down, but I guess my mouth was not closed completely because some sort of insect (Dr. Morton could probably identify it) flew into my mouth. I had noticed more bugs in the area around the bridge, and I must not have been cautious enough. After a few spits and sputters, I managed to eject the critter. It did have a sour taste, in case you were wondering.

Speaking of a headwind, today was our first day on this trip to have an actual headwind. It was from the southwest, and we were generally riding west, but we did have to fight against it on some of the roads that we travelled. I am thankful that the wind has been more of a help than a hindrance thus far.

Another exciting development was that my wife Jana travelled down by car to meet us today! She drove most of the day, but amazingly, as we were riding LA 10 and getting close to our turn, I actually saw her make the turn toward New Roads just before us. We were within eyesight of each other after coming from completely different directions with different modes of transportation. It astonished me.

The next two days will be rest days. Jana and I will do some exploring of the area, and we will make a trip to Baton Rouge for some bike store purchases. Bob is looking to replace his seat. I will still journal these rest days, but we will not add any distance riding.

One of the many rural churches on our route, this one near Slaughter, LA. We stopped here and found an outside faucet to fill our water bottles. Thanks!

Crossing the Mississippi River. This was a notable event on our journey, near New Roads, LA. The new bridge is very nice.

Day 14: March 15, 2015 - New Roads, LA - Rest Day

The random mystery word for yesterday was: stew. There will not be a mystery word today, since it was a rest day. Sorry folks.

Verse of the Day: "...set apart by the Spirit for obedience..." - a portion of 1 Peter 1:2. This was from Randy Osborne's sermon text at First Baptist Church, New Roads, Louisiana this morning. It was a friendly congregation and we enjoyed worshipping there.

So today was our first full rest day. I will just cover some of the highlights from Jana's and my adventures. We attended First Baptist Church in New Roads, and the guest pastor, who was a former pastor of that church, was from Broken Arrow, Oklahoma, and his wife was from Catoosa. We had a nice chat with him before and after the service.

From there, we headed over to St. Francisville. It is across the Mississippi River from New Roads. The town has a long history stretching back to the late 1700s. We stopped into the Historical Society and Museum and then enjoyed a walking tour on Royal Street. The city also hosts a three day festival in June that includes a reenactment called "The Day the War Stopped". Many plantations and historic homes are in this area.

We drove north a few miles to the community of Wakefield. It is always fun to see your last name on numerous town signs and buildings. On the way back south, we stopped at the Cottage Plantation for a tour. The plantation is very large, but not as well kept as many. It was an interesting tour nonetheless. I might recommend other options if you are in the area though.

Finally, we drove north on Highway 1 to check out the next leg of our bike route. We drove back on 905, which ran parallel to Highway 1. Highway 1 runs to Marksville, and will be our likely route. It has a good shoulder for all but a few miles. Dinner concluded the day. Tomorrow we head to Baton Rouge to check out a few bike shops. After our second rest day, we should be in good shape to get back on the bikes.

Grace Episcopal Church in St. Francisville, LA. It was damaged during the civil war, repaired in 1893. The organ dates to 1860.

Dinner at a restaurant overlooking the False River at sunset.

Day 15: March 16, 2015 - New Roads, LA - Rest Day #2

There will not be a mystery word today, since it was a rest day. Sorry folks.

So today was a second rest day in New Roads, Louisiana. We would not normally do two rest days in a row, but since my wife Jana was down we decided to take another day off. We did some sightseeing around Baton Rouge today.

First, we went to Mikey's Donuts for a great ham biscuit, donuts, and coffee. Then, Bob headed out with us to Baton Rouge bike shops. Our plan for today was to get our hands on one or two Brooks B-17 seats that everyone is raving about. We made a few calls on our way over, and ended up making our first stop at the Bicycle Crossing. Matt was a great help there, and Bob left with a B-17 saddle in his hands and at a good price too (under $130). But Bob did not find shorts he liked, and Matt recommended we check out The Bicycle Shop adjacent to the LSU campus. We drove over and the staff helped Bob locate shorts and better gloves, but they do not carry any Brooks saddles. They did have the Proofide saddle break-in oil or cream that is recommended by Brooks. That was odd. Two shops, two successes. But I was still interested in acquiring a saddle for myself. My backup option was to order one from REI, ship it home, and then pick it up in just over a week when went through northern Texas. We walked across the street to Massey's Outfitters. They are more than just a bike shop, and Andre was not even sure they carried Brooks seats. I looked around and spied one hanging high on the wall though. Success again. He gave us a bit of a discount, and I also had a B-17 for under $130 out the door. It took three shops, but we now had all of the items we were seeking that day.

By this time, we were interested in lunch. There were some excellent options right around campus, so we ended up eating at Raising Cain's Chicken Fingers. This location turned out to be the very first restaurant opened in 1996.

After lunch, we headed in the direction of the Louisiana State Capitol. This 450 foot tall structure opened in 1932 and is the tallest capitol in the United States. The observation deck on the 27th floor provides wonderful views of the city and the Mississippi River. At the welcome center, we talked with Dillan. He asked us where we were from, what we were doing, and other normal questions asked at visitor centers. He mentioned that he was from Franklinton. We were quick to describe our stop in Franklinton, including our lunch at the Fair City Cafe, and the gentleman who offered us a place in his pool house. Amazingly, Dillan explained that this was James Penny, and that he was friends with Mr. Penny's grandsons and had swam in that pool many times. Fascinating!

After touring the capitol, we headed back to New Roads, making a brief stop at the Pointe Coupee Museum and Visitor Center. The structure on the bank of the False River was an overseer cabin, constructed on that site in 1760, and it was the original structure. The ladies provided a great tour and a very interesting summary of the history of the area.

Back at the motel, we installed our new saddles, cleaned and lubricated our chains, and packed away some of our gear. The two rest days were very helpful, but tomorrow we ride!

Visiting the 450 foot tall Louisiana State Capitol in Baton Rouge.

A quaint bed and breakfast in Saint Francisville, LA.

Day 16: March 17, 2015 - New Roads to Marksville, LA - 52.2 miles

On the Road Again (as Willie Nelson would say)

70 degrees to start, 82 degrees to finish, partly sunny, 9:00 AM to 3:30 PM, winds W at 5 mph, 10.9 average mph, 24 mph max, 4:45 hours riding time. There was not a random mystery word yesterday, since it was a rest day, but there will be one today.

Verse of the Day: "A friend loves at all times..." - Proverbs 17:17.

Well, it seems like a week since I have been riding my bike. I know in my mind it has only been two days, but after nearly two weeks of daily riding, the two days off seemed longer than that. Perhaps that is a good thing.

We make a turn northwest today, since we will cross Texas north of Dallas. We are off of the Southern Tier route again. The best distance for today would be to Marksville, about 50 miles north of New Roads. We planned a bit later start, since Jana and I stayed at a bed and breakfast in St. Francisville last night. We wanted to look around yesterday in that historic town. Since the ferry has been replaced by the new bridge, bicycling through St. Francisville on a tour is not as convenient.

We departed the Cypress Inn in New Roads about 9:00 AM. That is a good option for anyone cycling through New Roads. Reasonable, clean, Wi-Fi, and a good location are all positive attributes for the Cypress Inn. The route today would keep us on Louisiana highway 1 all day. Jana was going to hang around New Roads a little longer to read, shop, walk and so forth before catching up to us for lunch.

Most of the route before lunch had a good shoulder. It was wide and in good condition. Much of the area was farmland and very flat. We rode up onto a long levee before Morganza, and had to cross a flood control structure. The highway bridge over the spillway was down to two lanes without any shoulder, and it was a long distance across the spillway. We were happy to find a narrow sidewalk just outside of the highway concrete barrier. It took a steady hand, but we crossed in time, separated from traffic.

Another interesting occurrence this morning was a yellow crop duster working a field to our east. We stopped to watch his acrobatics for a few minutes and to take a water break. We would end up seeing him flying on one side of the highway or the other a few more times today. We also stopped at a convenience store before lunch for a break. Bob had not eaten breakfast yet - someone should tell him it is the most important meal of the day. Oh wait, I have! He selected a fried corn dog and a mini pecan pie for his first meal of the day - to each his own.

The new seats were also feeling quite good. I have been told it will take 100 miles or so to break in a leather seat, but it was feeling better than the old one by the afternoon. I think we will be pleased with this investment. I noticed how much better it felt when we would make a stop, and then I would get back on the seat to start riding again. At this point, I could definitely tell it was more giving than the old seat.

We had a new experience before lunch. We were riding the shoulder, and a white pickup pulling a flatbed trailer loaded with white gravel, about an inch and a half in size, passed us. However, his flatbed did not have any sides, the load was too full, and it was not covered. As he hit bumps in the road, pieces of gravel were falling onto the roadway, taking big bounces at 65 mph, and both Bob and I were struck in the back or side by at least one gravel projectile. I do not know what he was thinking, but most likely he was simply not. No permanent damage was done, thankfully.

About 7 miles before Simmesport, which was our planned lunch stop, the shoulder turned to gravel, so we had to stay on the roadway. Traffic was moderate, but most drivers were considerate. We did not feel unsafe, just a bit squeezed from time to time.

Just before Simmesport, we had to cross a steep, tall bridge over the Atchafalaya River. This bridge was in the process of being repainted, so they only had one lane of traffic open. Our northbound lane was stopped by a flagman, so we rode up to ask him how he would like us to cross. Surprisingly, he said, "Ya'll can go". I told him to make sure we would not be hit, and he said we were fine. It took us a few minutes to climb the steep bridge, and there were a few work trucks changing positions, but we essentially had the entire bridge to ourselves. We said hello to the workers sitting at the edge eating lunch, and we were thrilled at the ease of our traverse of the bridge. The long line of traffic heading south that had to wait on us might not have been so happy, but we are legal vehicles on the road.

We soon arrived at Simmesport and selected the Family Grill for lunch. Jana had driven ahead to meet us, and we had delicious BLT and Club sandwiches. Lunch took a while, but we were glad to have the nourishment. It was also a nice break at about 33 miles. The day was starting to heat up.

We headed north on highway 1 again after finishing lunch. The temperature was around 80 degrees. The wind has been out of the west more or less, at about 5 mph. So we did have a headwind at times. The shoulder, however, took a turn for the worse. It was older asphalt with cracks that were harsh bumps to our bodies every ten or twelve feet. These are the stretches of road you have to grind through. We got onto the edge of the travel lane from time to time, but traffic was heavier and we spent most of our time taking a beating on the shoulder. As we got closer to Marksville, the shoulder improved.

Marksville was doing road construction, but for most of the area that had been reduced to one lane, we could simply ride on the inside of the orange cones. It turned out to be a good stretch to ride. We essentially had our own bike lane for a few miles.

Tonight, we found a room at the Terrace Inn Motel. It is an older motel, built in the 1960s, and probably remodeled in the 1980s. It is clean, though, and well kept. A room with a queen bed is only $50 + tax, not bad. The room has a desk, fridge, microwave, TV, hair dryer along with the usual suspects. Be warned, there is no Wi-Fi or breakfast. They do have morning coffee and a pool.

Tomorrow has a rainy forecast. We will have to decide on a short day to Alexandria, or attempt a long day to Natchitoches, Louisiana. Tune in tomorrow for these and other exciting destinations.

The Morganza Flood Control Structure in Louisiana diverts Mississippi River water during floods into the Atchafalaya Basin. It was opened during the 1973 and 2011 floods.

Entering Marksville, LA, a town of about 6,000. Established by Marc Eliche after his wagon broke down in this area.

Day 17: March 18, 2015 - Marksville to Alexandria, LA - 32.6 miles

A Nice, Easy Ride in the Country

70 degrees to start, 75 degrees to finish, partly cloudy, 9:30 AM to 12:30 PM, winds E at 5 mph, 11.9 average mph, 21 mph max, 2:45 hours riding time. The random mystery word for yesterday was: shop.

Verse of the Day: "The name of Yahweh is a strong tower, the righteous run to it and are protected." - Proverbs 18:10.

This was Jana's last morning with us, as she was heading home after breakfast. We ran back into town for a quick breakfast under the golden arches - Bob's favorite. We had placed our order and were standing back from the counter waiting. An older couple came in and approached Bob. They asked him, "Are you waiting in line?" To this Bob replied, "No, I haven't lost my mind." Never a dull moment. If that is not the quote of the day, then I do not know what should be. I think I laughed to myself for five minutes over that one.

The rain chances really were increasing this afternoon. We made the decision last night to start a little later, and only ride to Alexandria - less than 35 miles away.

Our next possible stop would make for an 85 mile day, which would be difficult in a pouring rain.

We were back on our originally planned route today. We left Marksville on Highway 107. Google bicycle routing also recommended this road, although they made some complex zig zags that we omitted. The road was quite good. Most of it had a decent shoulder, and the drivers were courteous. One of the occurrences that I have noticed on the shoulder is interesting. Often times, as I ride along through the small, pea gravel, my tire pinches a piece on the side and the pressure suddenly propels it quickly sideways. Today I heard a piece that was ejected clink off of a metal fence post. After this many miles, your brain finds odd things amusing.

We made our first of two crossings of the Red River in Louisiana today. Just north of Marksville, we crossed the swollen river on a nice long, gently sloping approach to the Red River bridge. We will cross it again in the next day or so. That may be our only crossings of the Red River by bicycle. I plan to be in Tishomingo sometime next week, but we have decided to leave the bikes on the route in Texas, and Jana will come and pick me up to go home for a day or so. It would be exciting to bike into the town where we live, but we are already riding so far north of the Southern Tier route that an additional detour into Oklahoma would add several more days to our trip. This option makes the most sense for me and my family at this time.

After the Red River, we continued riding northwest on 107. We were enjoying the rural road with green fields and numerous native pine trees. We made one interesting stop though. I must first explain that back in the 1980s, Bob and I would bicycle 30 miles southwest of Bartlesville, Oklahoma, to Woolaroc - a ride that included a 3 mile hill. On more than one occasion, I recall Bob stopping to help a small box turtle across the highway. It was just something he did. Well, this morning, we came upon a rather large snapping turtle in the road. You guessed it, Bob hit the brakes. However, I do not think that this snapping turtle was very appreciative of Bob's kindness. But I might have misinterpreted the hissing, clawing, and snapping! We rolled away with the turtle safely in the ditch.

We enjoyed the cool morning ride today. The clouds protected our skin from sunburn, and we had a slight tail wind, or perhaps no wind at all, much of the morning. The temperatures were nearly perfect, and the scenery was lovely. We made a stop to admire a rural mailbox along the highway with very nice purple petunias growing around the base. We also rolled past 800 total miles on this journey today. We are nearly one third of the way to the Pacific Ocean. It is hard to believe, even for us.

I would also like to provide a seat report. This is the second day on the Brooks B-17 leather saddle. It felt much better than yesterday. I was quite conscious of the seat yesterday, and it still felt very firm. Today, I forgot all about the new seat for most of the day. It seems to be breaking in nicely, with over 80 miles on that seat now. We also took the opportunity this afternoon to apply more of the Brooks Proofide treatment to the bottom of the leather seat. This is supposed to help the break in process. I expect the seat to feel even better tomorrow.

It has been starting to rain outside our window in Pineville, Louisiana, (next to Alexandria) this afternoon. It appears that our decision to ride for half of a day worked out well. We will use the afternoon constructively though. We already treated the new saddles, and we will do some route checking and planning to cover the next couple of days. I also need to reply to guestbook entries. Finally, we need to get to sleep early this evening. We will want to make an early start tomorrow, as we are hoping for no rain and a 70+ mile riding day.

The nice rural lane of Highway 107 between Marksville and Pineville, LA. Bob is trying to pick up and move the turtle, but it is not very understanding of the help he is being given!

My nearly broken in Brooks B-17 leather saddle. I forgot that it was under me for most of the day, which is a good sign.

Day 18: March 19, 2015 - Alexandria to Coushatta, LA - 75.7 miles

Our Longest Day Yet, Not Too Difficult It Was

60 degrees to start, 74 degrees to finish, partly cloudy, 8:00 AM to 4:00 PM, winds E at 4 mph, 12.2 average mph, 32 mph max, 6:10 hours riding time. The random mystery word for yesterday was: pea.

Verse of the Day: "Happy is the man who fears the Lord..." - Psalm 112:1a, seen on one of the many church signs we rode by today. An informal observation is that a majority of the small churches so far along our journey have been Baptist.

We knew this would be a long day, but we felt good after a short day yesterday. There were not a lot of lodging options on our route in this stretch, so our distance today was somewhat forced upon us. The weather forecast was good, and we were hoping for good roads. We even had a light tailwind at times.

We had a surprisingly good breakfast at the Sleep Inn in Pineville, Louisiana. When we checked in yesterday, we were told they had a "full" continental breakfast. We were delighted this morning to find scrambled eggs, sausage, waffles, boiled eggs, bananas, cereal, oatmeal, and so forth. This filling breakfast would put fuel in our tank for the long ride ahead of us. We were finished with breakfast and rolling out the front doors at 8:00 AM.

Yesterday, we followed a state route, but today we were on US Highway 71. I was concerned that we would encounter heavy traffic, but that was simply not the case. We had noticeably less traffic than yesterday, and most of the route had an excellent shoulder. In the areas with a poorer shoulder, we could ride in the traffic lane, and then shift over to the shoulder when we saw traffic in our mirror. This method works well with light traffic.

Our ride on US 71 today would generally follow the Red River valley. This corridor contains Interstate 49, which was far out of sight from us, LA state route 1, the river, US 71, and a rail line. We rode through the communities of Montgomery, St. Maurice, and Clarence, before reaching our destination of Coushatta.

Drivers were courteous again today. Most gave us plenty of room. At one point, a pickup slowed down and came up beside, us, matching our speed. This is the first time that has happened on our journey. He asked where we started and where we were headed. After we explained that we started in Georgia and were headed to California, his one word response was "Dang." He wished us luck, told us to be safe, and drove on his way. At least two vehicles gave us friendly honks and waves as they passed.

We made a mid-morning stop in Montgomery at a gas station. I grabbed a Gatorade and some peanut M&Ms, but Bob took his time to select something extra special from the wide selection of deep fried delights. He finally settled on the old standard, a corn dog. After some difficulty opening the mustard packet, he was in heaven. I am sure his fat cells were leaping with joy, as he puts it. But after a couple of bites, putting mustard on each bite before he ate it, something went horribly wrong and the next thing I know, he had mustard squirted all over his arm. Maybe this will be a good substitute for the sunscreen he is avoiding.

It was a really nice ride overall today. The clouds kept the sun of off us for much of the day, and the temperatures felt really wonderful. We were again riding across rural America, passing green fields, pine trees, small herds of cattle, blooming redbuds, and budding wildflowers. At one point we spied an entire field covered in yellow wildflowers, so much so that it practically glowed. We normally do not stop during an uphill climb, but we hit the brakes hard and took a short break to enjoy the wonderful view of creation.

On at least two occasions today, people on the side of the road greeted us or waved. One said good luck, and another wished us safety. It is encouraging to see the cheerfulness of strangers.

Lunch was at a local, well established BBQ place. Grayson's Barbeque has surely been in business for many years, judging by the building and the thousands of business cards taped to the wall. Seriously, business cards covered four walls in the place. The sliced ham sandwich on a homemade bun was very good, but I must say that it is the first time that I have seen a slice of pecan pie served in a sandwich bag. It is homemade, so do not let the package fool you.

Well, that about covers it for today. Tomorrow will be shorter, and we may encounter some rain. We will not make Texas by the end of tomorrow, but we will be very close. If you are taking on our mystery word challenge, I hope you are having some success. Sometimes we pick a new random word, if one we find is too difficult. Many words are hard to work in, such as snorkel, hospital, baboon, or wizard. Thanks for reading along with us. We will pass the 900 mile mark tomorrow.

A view back at Bob, pedaling along US 71 in Louisiana. The road, and shoulder, were very nice today.

A field covered in yellow wildflowers along our route on US 71 today. This was so amazing that we just had to stop and enjoy.

Day 19: March 20, 2015 - Coushatta to Greenwood, LA - 56.5 miles

We Were Blessed with Minimal Rain, Navigated Across Shreveport

65 degrees to start, 72 degrees to finish, misty drizzle then cloudy, 8:30 AM to 3:30 PM, winds NE at 8 mph, 10.6 average mph, 20 mph max, 5:15 hours riding time. The random mystery word for yesterday was: baboon.

Verse of the Day: "A man's steps are determined by the Lord, so how can anyone understand his own way?" - Proverbs 20:24

Today was supposed to be a 'normal' distance day. When we were trip planning, we were hoping to ride about 60 miles per day, 6 days per week. After a long 75+ mile ride yesterday, today's route was expected to be about 56 miles. There was some chance of rain today, but the amount was expected to be low.

The Budget Inn in Coushatta worked out fine last night, but they do not have breakfast. We walked across the street for breakfast biscuit sandwiches, orange juice, and coffee at Burger King. It was foggy, but not raining. We walked back to our room, finished packing, and rolled out just after 8:30 AM this morning. As we headed out to the street, we could feel the falling mist on our arms and faces. The temperature was quite nice at around 65 degrees.

Today's route would be on the other side of the Red River for most of the day. We took US Highway 84 north out of town, which was also LA Highway 1. We crossed the bridge over the Red River just beyond the edge of Coushatta, and it was full and out of its banks in the area around the bridge. LA 1 was a good route today, and much of the shoulder was average or better. This route is also not what we originally planned. Since we are not riding all the way to Oklahoma, we are turning west sooner than our initial plan. This has caused us to modify the route starting at Coushatta, Louisiana.

With all of the rain recently, most of the ditches along our route were full of water for miles. From time to time I could see a frog jump from the edge out into the water as our approach must have startled them. Speaking of frogs, yesterday we saw some guys using a wire basket on the end of a long pole, working the water in the ditches. I would guess that they were trying to catch frogs. I tried to convince Bob to eat some frog legs when we were in New Roads, but he was not interested.

We also saw our first drilling rigs this morning. After all of the miles that we have ridden, we saw our first two or three rigs along LA 1 south of Shreveport, Louisiana. We also were passed by many logging trucks (normal), and some drilling related trucks as well today. This was all along the Red River valley, heading northwest toward Shreveport.

Around noon, we were riding past an industrial park area on the south side of Shreveport. I understand that Shreveport was founded in 1836 by a development company trying to establish a town at the intersection of the Red River and the Texas Trail. The town soon became a focal point of steamboat commerce from the river.

After the route became four lane, we began to look for a place to acquire some nourishment. We had not seen anything, even a gas station, since the outskirts of Coushatta. We soon found a truck stop called the Relay Station. I am not normally one who dines at truck stops, but we were getting hungry. Surprisingly, the spicy chicken spaghetti and apple cobbler were quite good. Bob complimented the cashier on her brightly colored fingernails. I don't know if he was hoping for a discount or what, but we did not get one. Once our stomachs were full, we left, Gatorade in hand, and headed back to our bicycles.

Soon after lunch, the highway traffic was all moved to the west side of the median, as construction barriers blocked the east side lanes. This was once again to our benefit, since we were able to ride on the empty traffic lanes for more than a mile, up until construction equipment forced us over among the normal traffic. Drivers were again courteous today. Almost all gave us plenty of room, and we did not hear any angry horns.

Today was also extremely flat. We really did not encounter any hills until we were in Shreveport itself. From LA 1, we turned west on 511 or 70th street to head west across town. This road would take us all the way to Greenwood. It was four lane, but without any shoulder. We tried to stay as far right as possible, and traffic was careful to pass us when they could. The road curved down around the south end of the airport, and most of our hills were from the airport out to the motel. We were getting tired. We had a slight headwind today, and riding in traffic can also be taxing. We had to really watch our rear view mirrors and also the roadway for debris and obstacles. As I climbed one of the longest hills, having slowed to a crawl, I passed a mailbox with multiple bins. At my speed, I felt like I could have opened a mailbox door, and had time to insert a package or mail, never stopping my pedaling. It is strange what thoughts your brain entertains while spinning your feet.

Our destination today was the Mid Continent Inn. Interestingly, the motel was not on TripAdvisor, but it is the westernmost hotel available on our route before entering Texas. Upon check-in we learned they have full cable, which means that we should be able to watch both Oklahoma teams (OU and OSU) play basketball tonight! We also have several dinner options close by.

Tomorrow is very uncertain. The rain chances look quite high, but we will look it all over and make a plan. This is our nightly routine. We check the weather, check the maps, look for motels, and tweak our route. We are nearing 950 miles now on this journey. If the heavy rain holds off, we should be in Texas tomorrow. We are about five miles away now, but we must ride much further than that to find lodging.

One of our favorite road signs. We saw about four of these as we entered Shreveport, LA, from the south on LA Route 1.

We crossed over I-20 just before reaching our motel. We were grateful for the interstates. They suck up all the cars and leave the lesser highways emptier for us cyclists.

Texas

Day 20: March 21, 2015 - Greenwood, LA to Longview, TX - 50.5 miles

Rain AND Cold, and State # 6

56 degrees to start, 60 degrees to finish, rain all day, 9:00 AM to 3:45 PM, winds E at 7 mph, 10.8 average mph, 25 mph max, 4:40 hours riding time. The random mystery word for yesterday was: package.

Verse of the Day: "The one who pursues righteousness and faithful love will find live, righteousness, and honor." - Proverbs 21:21

It rained most of the night last night, and today's forecast called for rain again. We got up a few minutes later than usual, knowing that we would likely not ride a long day in the rain. Within walking distance was a Subway, and their breakfast sandwich provided much needed eggs and meat for the day's start. Back at the room, we looked at the radar and packed up our gear. It continued to rain, but it was not a downpour. We figured we could ride at least 25 miles today to Marshall.

We mustered up our courage and headed out into the rain. We started out right away with our rain jackets on, and I even had my sleeves on underneath. The temperature would stay in the upper 50s most of the day. Our route was relatively easy, navigationally speaking. We crossed I-20, picked up US 80 west, and pedaled on. It was a constant and cold rain from the first mile, but we simply kept ourselves moving forward.

After about 6 miles, we crossed from Louisiana into Texas. A new state would be one of the highlights of our day, and this would make our sixth state so far on our journey. It is hard to believe, even for us, that we have come this far in about three weeks. I was not sure if we would see a "Welcome to Texas" sign on this rural highway, but Texas did not disappoint. We pulled off for a couple of photos, but left on all of our rain gear.

US 80 was a good route today. It rolled past farms and pastures, and through a small town or two. We had a decent shoulder and sometimes the right lane when the highway became four lane. I would say the route was above average compared to what we have experienced. Drivers were again courteous and kind, with most of them moving over and giving us a wide berth. We enjoyed a few friendly honks and waves, even in the rain today. It is also possible they felt sorry for us, or thought we were idiots. But, I can say that the riding was not as bad to us as they probably imagined.

Not far into Texas, we made a stop at a convenience store in search of bananas. They did not have any, so peanut butter M&Ms were my substitute snack. As I was standing outside waiting on Bob to select some sort of artery-clogging preservative-filled treat, two gentlemen approached and asked where we were headed. They were Brian and Billy. It seems Brian is in his 50s and does triathlons. He was interested in the bike aspect of the tour, since he bikes. They were very friendly and I would say we chatted for 20 minutes or more about a variety of topics. It was a nice visit with a couple of strangers. Also, good luck in your new business, fellows.

The terrain of east Texas was hillier than Louisiana, but most were gentle and rolling hills. Before we knew it, we had put 25 miles behind us and were entering the edge of Marshall, Texas. The city has a population of over 20,000 and was apparently a political center of the Confederacy during the Civil War period. I also understand that Marshall has one of the largest light festivals in the United States and is the self-proclaimed Pottery Capital of the World.

We decided that since the rain was moderate, but not torrential, we would find a quick restaurant to eat lunch. I suggested that we eat at a new chain, somewhere we had not patronized on our trip thus far. With these requirements, we decided that the local Whataburger would do nicely. We parked our bikes under an eave to keep them out of the rain, since we do have leather seats now. Bob knew what to order before we reached the counter. He is quite the greasy burger connoisseur. One of the staff, Tommy, approached us and asked about our ride. He was very excited to hear that we were headed to California. I was really pleased with our lunch choice. The food was excellent, the staff were friendly, Christian music was on the radio, and the facility was clean. Thanks folks!

As far as the scenery today, we tried to take frequent looks, but the rain in our face made it difficult. We also had to watch traffic, and the road, since the wet pavement was more slippery. I did notice that fields were quite green, and flowering redbud trees again were present. A new shoulder hazard appeared today - sweet gum balls. Those hard, spiny, round balls from sweet gum trees were all over the shoulder at many locations. I had not seen them much before today. Odd.

A few miles west of Marshall, in the rolling hills of east Texas, we met Bruce. He was riding west, on a touring bike loaded with front and rear panniers. He crossed over to meet us. I am sure that he could see us from a mile away with our flashing headlights. He was headed to Greenwood, LA for the night - actually to the same motel we had left earlier this morning. This is apparently his fifth long distance ride, and we enjoyed our short visit. It is a rare occurrence to meet another bicycle tourer, especially this far north of the Southern Tier route. You can read more about Bruce's journey here: http://www.agentsofgaming.com/bikeabout5.htm

A couple of observations after a day in the constant rain. First, you really have to watch your speed down hills. I got up to 25 mph, but that was about as fast as I wanted to go, since the pavement was so wet. Also, you have to keep a sharp eye out for large puddles, deep standing pools of water, debris, rocks, mud, and so forth. All of these obstacles are also harder to see through the rain splattered glasses and on a road that has glare from being wet. And, since Bob is not running fenders, I had to be mindful of my lane position in order to avoid the rooster tail of water that would periodically come spewing from his back tire. It certainly made for an interesting day.

Actually, the day was quite a surprise. We were dreading the rainy ride before we left, and planned to cut it short, if needed. But, once we finished lunch, we both still felt really good. The rain was cold, but our constantly moving muscles generated enough body heat to keep us warm. I will admit that rain droplets hitting my jacket at 20 mph tended to force themselves through the fabric, so we were quite wet all over, and under, by the time the day was done. To me, it did not really feel like a 50 mile day, but that was what we ended up accomplishing.

We are showered and clean at our motel now, pondering our choices for dinner. Without a car, it limits our possibilities, so it might be Chinese food tonight - within walking distance. Tomorrow's plan will again depend on weather. I am trying to find a nearby church to go to worship in the morning. For tomorrow, Mineola looks good at about 45 miles away. We are satisfied with our progress today - 50 miles in the rain, and a new state.

Well, back from dinner now, and it was a Chinese Buffet that won out. Interesting note in my fortune cookie: Courage is not simply one of the virtues, but the form of every virtue at the testing point.

State number 6 on this grand adventure. We crossed the Louisiana-Texas state line about 6 miles in today on US 80.

It was hard to get many photos in the rain today. Here was a lone chimney, of a home of someone with a last name starting with "L", I presume. We appreciated the driveway to take a short break west of Longview, TX, on highway US 80.

Day 21: March 22, 2015 - Longview to Mineola, TX - 46.5 miles

1,000 Mile Mark, and Our First Flat

55 degrees to start, 65 degrees to finish, misting then cloudy then partly cloudy, 11:00 AM to 5:30 PM, winds N at 5 mph, 10.7 average mph, 30 mph max, 4:20 hours riding time. The random mystery word for yesterday was: courage.

Verse of the Day: "But I tell you, love your enemies and pray for those who persecute you..." - Matthew 5:44 from Dr. Cary Hilliard's sermon this morning at First Baptist Church in Longview, Texas.

I really wanted to go worship this morning, and Bob didn't mind some extra rest. It was also more likely to rain this morning, so a delayed start might be helpful. I texted my friend Sherman Aten, who has worked with churches all over Texas, to see if he had any suggestions for Longview. He did, but they ended up being about 5 miles away from our motel. This was a longer round trip than I wanted to ride. So, I looked and found FBC Longview, which was in the downtown area, just over a mile from our motel.

About 9:00 AM, I hopped on the bike in my "street clothes" and rain jacket. It was pretty informal for church, but it would have to do. We do not carry many clothing options with us. It was cloudy and misting, but not too heavy. It only took about 15 minutes to ride over to the church, so I made it in plenty of time for the 9:30 service.

First Baptist Longview is an older church, in the downtown area, and I would guess that the sanctuary was built in the 1960s. The ceiling was extremely tall, much like a cathedral. They had a guest guitar ensemble joining in the music this morning, from East Texas Baptist University in Marshall. They were very talented, and the style leaned toward bluegrass. I really enjoyed singing praises to those arrangements. I read online that Dr. Hilliard is from Duncan, Oklahoma and attended Oklahoma Baptist University.

The early service time worked for us, and I was leaving the church around 10:45. I headed back to the motel and we packed and left just before the 11:00 AM check out time. This was our latest start to date, but we only had about 46 miles planned for the day. I think Bob enjoyed the leisurely pack up time this morning. The radar showed that all of the rain had pushed east, but we did end up riding in a light mist for the first hour or so this morning.

We were back on highway US 80 headed west again today. During the ride, the day seemed very uneventful, but looking back as I type, we did have quite a few interesting things happen today. Most of the day was over rolling, gentle hills. The landscape was quite rural. At times we were beside green fields, and at other times tall pine trees lined our path. Most of the roadway was two lane, but we always had a decent shoulder or right lane when the highway went to four lane. Traffic was moderate, but not too heavy.

Just a mile or so down the road this morning, we rode passed the 1,000 mile mark on this grand adventure. We actually did not realize it until a few miles later. We are estimating 2,500 miles, since we are not riding into Oklahoma, so we are about 40% of the way to the Pacific.

After about 7 miles, we pulled into a grocery store in Gladewater in search of bananas. We each had a banana, and stowed two more for later. We decided to push on a bit further for lunch. After a couple of hours and about 22 miles of pedaling, we rolled into the town of Big Sandy, which is, ironically, quite small. We found Milano's Pizza, and decided that sounded very good. It was an interesting restaurant. When you go inside, it is connected to the Mexican restaurant next door. When being seated, we were asked if we wanted a Mexican or Pizza menu. I suppose having choices is nice. We opted for Pizza - Chicken Alfredo Supreme to be exact. It was delicious. The only problem was leaving. The restaurant was quite warm inside, and when we walked out into the 55 degree moist air, I suddenly wished that I was on a tropical Hawaiian island somewhere, basking in the sun.

As we headed back west, we rode by the International Alert Academy. I commented that some of the drivers that did not give us much space needed to enroll in a few courses there. After some assistance from Google, it appears this is a Christian disaster relief training organization at the former campus of Ambassador College. ALERT is an acronym for Air Land Emergency Resource Team.

Our last big news for today was that we had our first flat. We are actually feeling lucky that we have ridden on a total of four tires, over 1,000 miles each, and just now had to deal with a flat. It was Bob's back tire, and when inspecting it, there was a small piece of wire that we found and removed. We pumped it back up, and it held pressure for about four miles. We decided that it would be much easier to fix at the hotel room, using water in the sink to find the hole. So, we just made a quick stop four or five more times and pumped it back up to get us on into Mineola.

We timed ourselves on fixing the flat this evening, and not counting finding and patching the hole, it took 15 minutes from start to finish. We pulled the tube, located the hole, applied a patch, and let it dry. We then inspected the inside of the tire to make sure that nothing sharp was still embedded in the rubber. Then, we put it all back together and installed the wheel on the bike. If we had to deal with this on the road, we would just put in a new tube and get back to riding. We would then deal with the leaking tube later that night. So, our experience tells us that it would take about 15 minutes on the road, but we would get our hands quite greasy.

We are in Mineola, Texas, tonight. The town has a population of just over 5,000 and came into existence when the railroads built lines through east Texas in the late 1800s. Tomorrow, we change highways and take US 69 northwest, headed for Greenville. Today also marked being on the ride for exactly three weeks. We are hoping for sunny skies and tailwinds tomorrow.

We encountered some interesting odors as we pedaled by this soil and fertilizer plant east of Mineola, TX, on US 80.

The International ALERT Academy, on the edge of Big Sandy, TX. We might all benefit from more alertness.

Day 22: March 23, 2015 - Mineola to Greenville, TX - 50.1 miles

Flatter Hills, Approaching the Metro Area

57 degrees to start, 77 degrees to finish, clear and sunny, 9:00 AM to 2:30 PM, winds SE at 7 mph, 12.0 average mph, 36 mph max, 4:10 hours riding time. The random mystery word for yesterday was: island.

Verse of the Day: "Apply yourself to discipline and listen to words of knowledge" - Proverbs 23:12

We had a good breakfast at the Best Western in Mineola this morning. There were many hot options, but the waffle, sausage, eggs, and coffee were just right for me. My only complaint, being an Oklahoma native, was that I had to stare at a waffle in the shape of Texas. But that waffle did not last long.

Our day was only planned to be 50 miles, so we waited until 9:00 AM to depart. It was in the 40s when we woke up, but by the time we rolled out, it was in the upper 50s and the sun made it feel much warmer. We did make a quick stop and get a photo of the Mineola train station and a caboose before we left town.

We are still deviating from our original route today. We will not be back on our originally planned route until somewhere west of Decatur, Texas. We changed highways in Mineola, turning toward the northwest and taking US 69 towards Greenville. Small communities on our route today included Alba, Emory, Point, and Lone Oak. I was pleasantly surprised at the quality of the route for today's ride. I was afraid that US 69 would be loaded with heavy traffic, but I believe that the traffic was lighter than what we experienced on US 80 the last couple of days. Both the roadway and the shoulder were very good for nearly all of the day. We did not have any problems from drivers either.

Much of the day was spent pedaling past ranches and pastures, fields and farms. At one point, a small herd of about 30 cattle were watching intently was I rode by. A couple of calves were jumping around their mothers. I suppose I startled them at some point, because in a minute, one by one, they all started running away from the road. Was it something I said? I guess I will never know.

We were just west of Emory at 25 or so miles today, and it was nearly noon. We pulled off to a grassy area and removed our four pieces of leftover pizza from the panniers. The pizza was very good last night, and was still very tasty for lunch today. We also had pizza for lunch yesterday. It is starting to look like pizza is a staple of our diet, but I will try to find something different tonight. We did stop at another historical marker after lunch, and it was much more interesting than yesterday's marker. This one was near Ginger, Texas, which was not even on my map!

We detoured off of the highway in Point and rode on a side access road for a mile or so. I thought it might be too early in the season, but we are starting to see patches of bluebonnets along the side of the road today. We took a few minutes to enjoy them, and take a photo. It has been a beautiful and sunny day, and I certainly feel blessed by it.

The hills did not seem as steep as yesterday, but perhaps it was the slight tailwind that was helping us. There were a few nice hills this morning, and I was able to attain some fun speeds on a couple of descending runs. I also think that the shoulder was slightly better than yesterday. The warmer temperatures were an additional bonus. We had a good ride to Greenville, which was about as far as we could reasonably go and still catch a motel. The flat that we fixed yesterday is holding fine on Bob's bicycle.

We are staying in Greenville, Texas, tonight, a town on I-30 with a population of around 27,000. It was established in 1846 and named after a contributor who helped to establish Texas as a Republic, Thomas Green.

The sun should be on us again tomorrow, but the wind may change from a tailwind to a cross wind. That may slow our pace slightly. We may try to get an earlier start. Speaking of winds, the prevailing thought is that the wind will blow from west to east, so cross country tours should be done from west to east to take advantage of that wind. I need to go back and check my notes, but I would estimate that we have only had a noticeable headwind three or four days in total. I will keep track over the course of the entire trip to see how it works out for us.

The plan for tomorrow night is for my wife Jana to come down and pick me up in Texas. That will allow me to be home for two nights, before returning to ride again on Thursday. I think Bob plans to sleep for 36 hours in a motel while I am gone. He very well might; this guy can lay down on rocky asphalt and feel refreshed after five minutes. I am astonished every time I see it happen.

The train station in Mineola and a caboose, less than a mile from our hotel in Mineola, TX, on US 69.

The bluebonnets are making an appearance. Near Point, TX, on US 69 east of Greenville.

Day 23: March 24, 2015 - Greenville to Denton, TX - 66.7 miles

Traffic, Wind, and Traffic

60 degrees to start, 80 degrees to finish, clear and sunny, 8:00 AM to 4:30 PM, winds S at 20 to 30 mph, 10.8 average mph, 27 mph max, 6:10 hours riding time. The random mystery word for yesterday was: staple.

Verse of the Day: "Don't envy evil men..." - Proverbs 24:1a

Last night's dinner was at Arby's. It was a short ride from the Royal Inn. I went for the Market Fresh turkey and Swiss cheese, and Bob devoured three junior roast beef sandwiches. We were both tired and turned in early.

Some days are tranquil and serene, riding by open fields, tree lined lanes, a gentle wind behind you, cool breezes all around - and then there was today!

Actually, it was not all bad. Our motel did not offer breakfast, so we packed up and rode across to McDonalds. This time, I knew what I wanted before Bob - the big breakfast, pancakes, orange juice, and coffee. It was a good boost to get me started. We rode about half of a mile and turned west on US 69 / 380. We will follow US 380 all the way to Roswell, New Mexico, so we will know the road well by then.

The ride on US 380 from Greenville to Farmersville and even on to the edge of McKinney was quite nice. We had smooth surfaces and good shoulders. The Lavon Lake water level, west of Farmersville, certainly looked to be very low. I guess they are needing some rain. Along the way that first half of the day, I saw a hawk - one of the first on this trip, as odd as that sounds. We see them all the time in Oklahoma. Also, in a field with three cows, there was a llama - I almost did not notice him among them. I have seen a few llamas in the last three weeks.

I knew from the forecast that we may have a decent crosswind from the south. It started strong and became stronger as the day wore one. At one point I felt like I was wearing out the sidewall of my tires from riding tilted into the wind. The crosswind did not actually slow us down as much I had expected though. At times, the road would angle north, and we would have a slight tailwind. At other times, it felt more in our face, but it was never demoralizing or overbearing.

Once we reached McKinney, it became more tense and difficult. It was surprising to me that a town of 150,000+, close to a metro area, where you might think bicycling would be popular, would build a road with NO shoulders. Six lanes, a white line, eight inches, and then a curb of all things. However, in Prosper, the shoulder came back, but construction had torn it out and put up large barriers, again leaving us with no room to ride.

I will say that 99.9% of the drivers were very courteous and gave us an entire lane. The 0.1% would be the black Pontiac two door that blared a horn at us, I suppose because we were not over in the field pedaling through tall grass, who knows. I never felt in danger or peril though. I do think God is helping me to learn more patience on this journey.

We were almost through Prosper when a patrol car came up behind us with the lights on. We were in the section with barriers for construction, so there was not a place to get off the road. We just stopped in our lane, as did the police car. He was concerned about our safety while biking on that road. We explained what we were doing, and that we had researched google maps and were expecting a shoulder. He let us know that the shoulder was available again at the top of the next hill and he followed us up to that point for extra safety. We appreciated Officer Jones' concern. This is one reason why we use the rear view mirrors - we can keep a cautious eye on traffic from behind. I am quite sure that I spent more time staring at that rear view mirror today than anything else.

The real issue is these larger towns building roads with zero room on the side for bikes. We were even on sidewalks in McKinney a few times, which I do not like to do. But even the sidewalks were few and far between. Bicycling this distance gives you an appreciation and awareness of issues that might normally be out of mind.

On a day like today, it is very difficult to see much of the scenery. We spent all of our time watching the rear view mirror for traffic behind, and then glancing forward to dodge trash at the pavement edge. But this trip has days like this - days that are not glamourous, and are tense and mentally challenging. This was such a day, but we know that the next day, or the day after that, will be different - and I look forward to it.

We made it to Denton, Texas tonight. My friend Bob is resting in a motel there; he decided not to come to Tishomingo with me. My wife Jana met us at the motel and picked me up. Actually, she let me drive home to Tishomingo, Oklahoma, where I will be for a day or two. It is strange driving a car again. After three or more weeks travelling at 10 to 15 mph, I find myself driving quite slow compared to the rest of the traffic. I have become used to things passing me by much more slowly. Also, I was on the bicycle seat for nearly eight hours today - and the leather saddle is working very well. I cannot explain it, but I am experiencing it. I found that sitting in the car seat for two hours this evening was actually more uncomfortable than eight hours on the bike today. I cannot explain that one either.

Tomorrow I will rest, or should I say work on a to-do list. But I am feeling good and like to keep busy. Then, in a day or so, I will travel back to Denton by car, and Bob and I will start biking west again. I think that we are almost exactly half finished with our grand adventure. So far, so good. Thanks to all for their prayers.

Welcome to Farmersville, TX. I suppose the name is fitting in the sea of farms and fields. I am all in for the farmers produce, but will pass on whatever the fleas have to offer.

No, I did not use extra starch in my flags last night. It is our slight crosswind today, 20 to 30 mph, on US 380 between Greenville and McKinney, TX.

Day 24: March 25, 2015 - Tishomingo, Oklahoma - 0 miles

A Rest Day at Home

Verse of the Day: "I am at rest in God alone, my salvation comes from Him." - Psalm 62:1

So we are resting from riding today. Bob is in Denton, Texas, and I am in Tishomingo, Oklahoma. It looks like we will rest one more day tomorrow, and then get back to riding on Friday.

Today was a good day to catch up on items that needed to be done around the house. I installed a hitch that I had ordered for our Honda Fit. I also trimmed bushes, mulched leaves and mowed the lawn. The tropical aquarium needed to be cleaned, and I was able to get that done. Jana and I enjoyed lunch at Gonzalez (Mexican food).

I was able to do a few trip related tasks also. I washed all of our clothes that were being carried with us. They get washed nearly every day, but a good cleaning at home was nice. I went through most of my gear, took a survey of what was needed and what was not, and pulled out some things to leave behind. I intend to be as light as possible before we start over the mountains.

This afternoon, Jana and I headed up to church to cook the Wednesday meal, and we enjoyed food, fellowship, and study with our church family. We rounded out the night with a nice long walk with our friends Dustin and Nicole. It was a good day.

I will wrap up a few more tasks tomorrow, look ahead at our route, and prepare for getting back on the bike on Friday. It has been great to see the family and sleep in my own bed. Goodnight all.

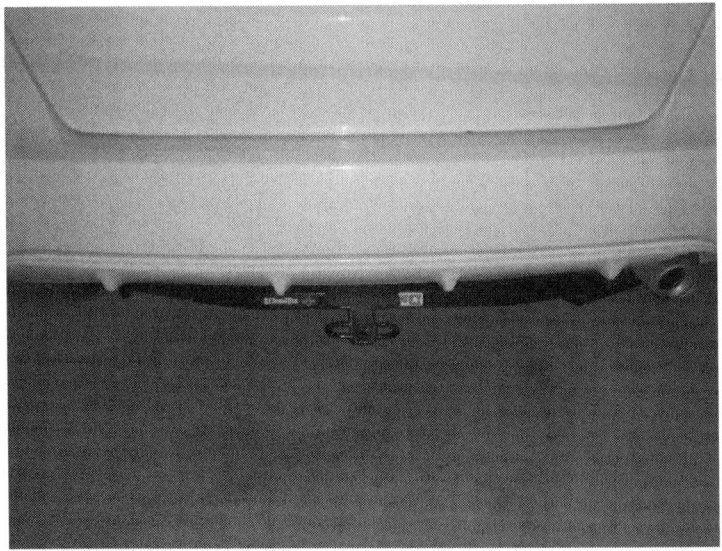

I installed the new hitch on the Honda Fit this morning. Now I can use it to carry my bike rack and bikes.

The sun is shining and the tank is clean. My fish should be happy for a few weeks until I finish the ride. Tim or Micah will keep them fed.

Day 25: March 26, 2015 - Tishomingo, Oklahoma - 0 miles

Rest Day #2 at Home

Another rest day... I was in Tishomingo, Oklahoma enjoying the day with family. Bob was in Denton, Texas, getting another day of R&R (rest and recovery). Bob, I hope you have been eating and drinking well, getting plenty of food and beverages!

The secret mystery word for yesterday was: survey.

Nothing major to report today, so this will be a short journal entry. I took care of a few extra things around the house today, so that maybe my wife won't have to worry about them too soon.

The girls are out at a club meeting, and I am waiting on my son Tim to get back from a track meet. Then, we can eat home-made pizzas and watch M*A*S*H. What more could you ask for this evening for a boys' night?

Tomorrow morning, we are back on the bikes heading west from Denton. Thanks to everyone who has been keeping up with us and praying for and encouraging us. It is very much appreciated.

Day 26: March 27, 2015 - Denton to Jacksboro, TX - 63.8 miles

I'm Back in the Saddle Again

58 degrees to start, 68 degrees to finish, clear and sunny, 9:00 AM to 4:30 PM, winds N then NE at 10 mph, 10.6 average mph, 28 mph max, 6:00 hours riding time. The random mystery word for yesterday was beverages.

Verse of the Day: "Don't abandon your friend or your father's friend..." - Proverbs 27:10a

While out on the road, especially if Bob and I are separated by much space, random songs tend to pop into my head. Today's theme could certainly be the tune by Gene Autry that played in my head this morning: "I'm back in the saddle again, out where a friend is a friend, where the longhorn cattle feed..." After two days off, I think we were both ready to put in a good day of riding.

I debated on whether to make our next day back after two rest days a full day or partial day. Yesterday, I got online and reviewed maps of the planned route from

Denton to Phoenix. I searched for all motels along the route to identify what towns were possible stops. I compared that to the distances between each town and the total elevation change and elevation change per mile. I also typed up a list and printed it on my laser printer so that we can have it for quick reference. The weather and wind are still big unknowns, but I was able to guess at some possible daily distances. It made the most sense with that information in hand to do a full day today. I am very glad we did, 64 miles and we are still feeling very good.

My wife Jana, her mom, and I left Tishomingo around 7:15 this morning. That put us meeting Bob at the motel just before 9:00 AM. We packed up our last few items, he loaded a box of gear to go back home with Jana in our car, and we left just after 9:00 AM headed west (again).

US 380 west of Denton was undergoing construction, so we checked the maps and jogged about a mile north to get on Jackson Road. This rural road ran parallel to US 380 for about 8 miles. Although almost all of it was paved, we did hit a patch of gravel for about 1/4 mile. This alternate road was a nice change of pace, with very little traffic, and many ranches along that road. One, the Three Forks Ranch, I believe, had several ornate gates. See the photo below. Also on Jackson Road, we were passed by a fellow, probably in his 30s, riding a mountain bike. It appeared that he was riding to or from a job. After he passed, I asked Bob how it felt to be passed by a guy on a mountain bike, who was also wearing jeans and work boots. He was not a cross country bicyclist, or if he is, he is tougher than I am.

Soon, our rural lane ended, and we were back on US 380. By now, the construction zone was nowhere to be seen, and we had a fantastic shoulder all the way to Decatur. The fields along the way were becoming quite green, and it would seem that this area of Texas has had a least some rain lately.

We stopped at a gas station between Denton and Decatur. Bob already had a Gatorade that we shared, so I bought a couple of packs of peanut M&Ms. The young girl at the checkout asked if we were biking, and to where. After I gave her our usual answers, she said that she would like to get in shape and do a long bike ride. I told her that she should just start riding, and the trip would get her in shape! She seemed excited for us, and she wished me well as I left.

As we approached Decatur, we had to decide whether we wanted to get off of the bypass and go into town for lunch, or continue on to Bridgeport. We really wanted to put at least half of the day's miles behind us before lunch, so we opted to continue around Decatur and expected to eat lunch at Bridgeport. We could see the old courthouse in town up on the hill. The courthouse was completed in 1896, and sits on the highest point of elevation in the county. Another interesting fact was that Dallas Baptist University (DBU) was founded in Decatur in 1898 as Decatur Baptist College and moved to Dallas in 1965. We did make a rest stop at the Decatur Civic Center on the northwest edge of town. The facility looks quite new, and I appreciated their strong Wi-Fi signal that allowed me to check my email from the parking lot!

We soon had 35 or so miles behind us and stopped in Bridgeport for Chicken Express. It was quite tasty, and the staff were happy to fill up our water bottles before we left. Thanks, ladies.

The landscape started to become markedly drier and more barren between Decatur and Bridgeport. The water level at Lake Bridgeport seems extremely low. All around the shore you can see boat ramps that no longer enter the water. All of the boat docks are sitting on the dry shoreline. They appear to really need a good amount of rain here.

On the west side of Bridgeport Lake, near Runaway Bay, we rode by the turn to Sid Richardson Scout Ranch. This was the Boy Scout summer camp destination for our troop last year. Doug and I took the boys in Troop 100 there, although water sports were challenging with the low lake level.

The terrain required considerably more hill climbing within 10 or 12 miles of Jacksboro. One long hill had us in our lower gears, plugging along at 5 or 7 mph for about 2 miles total. It reminded me of the "3 mile hill" outside of Bartlesville on the way to Woolaroc. I am certain it was our longest climb on the trip thus far. We will learn to embrace these climbs, because there are many more ahead of us. We are essentially starting a slow and steady elevation gain to cross the mountains in New Mexico. Even Roswell, New Mexico, is at about 3,600 feet. Our net elevation gain today from just Denton was about 400 feet.

One interesting landmark, not very far east of Jacksboro, was a water tower. Now, I have seen several municipal water storage tanks today, but this was different. This tank was up in the air, above the tree line, and it appeared to be on a private ranch. Unfortunately, the tower was quite far from the road, and my camera did not get an adequate photo. It was a white tank, with a red OU painted in several places around the tank. That must be a dedicated Sooner fan to put up an OU water tower in the middle of Texas. I was impressed.

Overall, we had a very satisfying ride today. The wind was sometimes a cross wind, then a head wind, and even rarely a tail wind. The day was beautiful, and the temperatures were cool and comfortable. I do not think I even worked up a sweat. Even with our later than usual start, we completed the day at a reasonable time.

We walked down the street to a local establishment for dinner - the Green Frog Restaurant. It has apparently been in business for quite some time. We had a solid, home cooked meal that included vegetables. At least I did. Bob selected mashed potatoes and fried onion rings for his vegetables. I told him that I don't think they count as vegetables.

We are now back in the room at the Butterfield Motel. It is #1 of 2 hotels in Jacksboro on TripAdvisor. Yeah, sometimes first place is not too difficult to attain. This has to be the smallest motel room that I have ever stayed in. We barely squeezed the bikes in, but may be tripping over them every time we move around tonight. But, for under $60 with Wi-Fi, we will make it work. We have cable TV so that we can watch OU play basketball tonight. That's worth the price of admission right there!

A couple of other items that I would like to update. First, the Malibu that we drove east to start this crazy trip has been sold! A big thank you to my friend Ron, and his friend Steve, both in Knoxville. I really appreciate them being willing to take that on. I am still amazed that we ended up getting to the east coast by driving a car out and selling it.

Secondly, my bike computer or speedometer magnet has been replaced. This item failed in Louisiana. It became loose, and would not tighten and stay tight. The magnet tells the sensor when the wheel has made one revolution. The computer is a Planet Bike Protege 9.0 model, and I really like this one because it has a four line display and includes the temperature. I emailed Planet Bike customer service, and Kristin Wentworth in their customer service department responded quickly. When I returned home last Tuesday night to see the family for a couple of days, a package was there with a new magnet and a bonus pair of free socks. Thanks, Planet Bike, for great customer support! Although my pink duct tape roadside repair was more eye catching, I think the new magnet that is now installed puts my mind at ease.

That is about all for today. I feel very blessed by the weather and our progress. Tomorrow may be warmer, so we will try to get an earlier start.

One of the interesting ranch gates on Jackson Road, west of Denton. This road was our alternate to US 380 for a few miles.

US 380 west of Denton, Texas. Nice shoulder.

Day 27: March 28, 2015 - Jacksboro to Throckmorton, TX - 65.9 miles

A Long.... Hot Day

52 degrees to start, 86 degrees to finish, clear and sunny, 8:00 AM to 5:30 PM, winds SSW at 8 mph, 10.1 average mph, 28 mph max, 6:30 hours riding time, net elevation change +236 feet. The random mystery word for yesterday was laser.

Verse of the Day: "Happy is the one who is always reverent..." - Proverbs 28:14a

We had really good intentions this morning to start early and avoid the heat. We left the Butterfield Inn motel in Jacksboro around 7:30 to head to Subway for a quick breakfast sandwich. We have eaten breakfast at Subway a few times, and I like the egg, meat, and spinach ingredients that I can have on my sandwich there. However, as we rolled into the parking lot, we realized that this Subway did not open for breakfast. But, right next door, there was a Dairy Queen that did serve breakfast. We made a quick turn and parked our bikes. We decided not to lock them... who in their right mind gets up early on Saturday morning to go steal a bike?

We struck pay dirt on the breakfast restaurant choice. Bob ordered some measly sausage biscuit, but I went for the country breakfast - two pancakes, two sausage patties, and two eggs over medium - just the way I like it. And it all was served on an antique china plate. How about that? The local Saturday coffee crowd and bull session was going full steam. Some discussion about inspection stickers and parking laws was keeping everyone riled up. Welcome to small town Texas.

We finished breakfast and headed back to the center of town in order to turn west again on US 380. As we began, Bob was riding quite slowly. I figured it was his tiny breakfast. I mean, he was trudging along at 6 to 7 mph. I was trying to be patient, thinking that he was just slow to get started. After about two miles, he asked me to look at his tires. The back tire was going flat, or was nearly flat. We pulled over and got off onto a gravel parking nearby. We pulled the tire, removed the tube, and checked the tire for anything still embedded in it. The tire felt good, so we just used one of the spare tubes that we were carrying, saving the bad one to patch later. We installed the new tube, and began pumping it up. At about 60 psi, we heard a "pop" and it lost all of the air. At first, I thought my pump had failed. After looking it all over, the tube had burst. I have heard of people getting bad tubes, so we pulled our second and only other spare tube out and installed it in the tire. Once it was assembled, we started pumping it up. At about 70 psi, to our horror, we heard a similar "pop" and the tire lost all air. Now we are in trouble.

Our spare tubes are shot, and the original tube has a leak. Leaks are more difficult to repair on the side of the road without any water basin to submerge the leaking tube in. We decided to use our drinking cup. I poured water in from my bottle, and we folded small sections of the tube and submerged them in the cup. After we tested about half of the tube, we found one small pin hole that was leaking. We checked the rest of the tube and it appeared fine. I broke out my patch kit and we patched the location of the hole. We assembled the tire with the original, patched tube, and pumped it back up. All now appeared to be in good shape. Our spare tubes were slightly smaller than the tubes currently being used. I had read of people using smaller tubes, saying they would just inflate more to fill the tire. Our setup apparently did not like the smaller tubes. We will need to locate new spare tubes as soon as we can. If we have a catastrophic tube or tire failure, we will be in bad shape.

We were now back on the road, headed to Graham, but the tube issues cost us over an hour of cool morning riding time. Our day just became longer. We did see a large group of wind generators on the west side of Jacksboro. I forgot to mention them yesterday. There was some partial headwind on the way to Graham, but not terrible. We stopped before Graham at a convenience store for Gatorade and some snacks. Traffic was moderate on the way to Graham. We arrived in Graham around noon, but with only 27 miles behind us. Subway was right on the corner, so we stopped in for a quick lunch. After polishing off my foot long, we filled our water bottles before heading out again. This particular Subway was different than most - it had a drive through, and if you dined in, your sandwich came in a basket, not a bag.

I did some route checking during lunch, and we decided to try Texas state highway 61 from Graham around the south side of Lake Graham. This route would save us two miles, and then it would connect with US 380 again in about 12 miles. We really enjoyed the state highway. Traffic was extremely light, and it was a nice change of pace. TX 61 also took us by Fort Belknap. This fort was established in 1851, became a stop in the Butterfield mail route, and was abandoned in 1867 due to an unreliable water supply. I suppose water issues are nothing new.

Once we rejoined US 380, we were surprised to find that traffic had nearly vanished. The rest of the day had extremely light traffic. It was also interesting to notice that some areas of the landscape appeared greener out here. Although the landscape was not consistent. At a few places, we saw green pastures, with grass a foot high, and grazing cattle enjoying a meal. A few miles later, the prickly pear cacti were so thick that you might think it was a cash crop. Overall, it was quite desolate. Not a gas station for the second 40 miles of our day.

The afternoon temperatures were climbing into the 80s, and on the black asphalt, my bike computer was registering a temperature of 97 degrees. Part of this reading was due to being in the sun, but as Bob pointed out, so were we. At one of our rest breaks along the side of the road, we had a pickup truck stop to ask if we were ok or needed any help. This was the first time a motorist has stopped to check on us during a break. We appreciated the gesture. At one point during this stretch of road, we met a guy on a bike headed east. We stopped for a quick chat. Jeff was headed to town, riding a bike with huge saddle bags. It was odd that he was wearing jeans and no helmet, but said that he was planning a cross country ride starting in May. I was intrigued, because starting any cross country ride from Texas in May seems crazy. Perhaps we misunderstood.

We stretched our water in our bottles, and rolled into Throckmorton about 5:30. We pulled into a gas station in town, at the one stoplight, and bought a couple of bottles of cold water and two bananas. As a coincidence, after we walked out of the store, a lady was walking in wearing a Pink Pistol T shirt from Tishomingo. I asked her if she had been to Tishomingo, and she said a relative picked it up for her. We then checked into the Double T Lodge - it looks much worse on the outside than on the inside. They took pity on Bob and gave us a nice discount on a room with two double beds. He was pretty beat from the day, having trouble writing his signature on the credit card receipt.

Before we could get into the room, the two good old boys checking us in had to remove their tools and vacuum around the door. They told us that they had been working on the door to that room. As they removed their tools, and their two beer cans that had apparently been keeping them from getting thirsty, we thanked them for the hospitality.

An update on the spare tube situation... Bob has contacted a friend in Phoenix who works on bikes. Randy has picked up two more tubes of the correct size and put them in the mail to us. We had them sent general delivery to a town about two days ahead. That will allow us to only have to ride a couple of days without a spare tube.

After refreshing showers in our room decorated with oilfield decor (maybe that did not sound right), we headed over to the Country Cafe, one of the two eating establishments in town. It is also not much to look at, but the home cooked meal was quite good. We are feeling much better now that we are clean and fed.

So tonight we are in Throckmorton, Texas - a town of about 800 people. They have a very nice old courthouse in the middle of town, and reportedly have a good six man football team in their high school. We are really going to try to start early tomorrow and avoid some of the afternoon heat.

Wind power generators just west of Jacksboro, TX, on US 380.

Our lonely TX 61 route. This was nice. Cars only came by every 10 minutes or so. West of Graham, TX.

Day 28: March 29, 2015 - Throckmorton to Aspermont, TX - 64.8 miles

Another Long.... Hot Day, but Better

58 degrees to start, 86 degrees to finish, clear and sunny, 7:30 AM to 5:00 PM, winds SW at 8 mph changing to N at 15 mph, 9.4 average mph, 23 mph max, 6:50 hours riding time, net elevation change +463 feet. The random mystery word for yesterday was signature.

Verse of the Day: "The wind blows where it pleases, and you hear its sound, but you don't know where it comes from or where it is going. So it is with everyone born of the Spirit." - John 3:8

We attempted another early start today, departing the "lodge" at 7:30 AM, knowing that it once again would get hot in the afternoon. We headed west out of Throckmorton on US 380. With our early start, and the tiny town we were in, I was hoping to catch an evening worship service at a church in our destination city.

Once again, US 380 was a very nice ride. The traffic was extremely light, just as it had been yesterday. We were dealing with a partial headwind this morning, as it blew from the southwest. About 8 or 10 miles out, Bob noticed that his tire was losing air pressure. Another flat - two days in a row, and we did not have any spare tubes.

We had to fix this one sitting on the shoulder, so we felt blessed that traffic was so light. This time, we ended up removing the tire completely from the rim, instead of just one side. While I got out the pump and water cup to try to find the hole, Bob checked over the inside of the tire very carefully. We do this every time we fix a flat, but a close inspection revealed a tiny piece of wire just protruding through the inside of the tire. Using our small cup of water, we located the small pinhole on the tube. This was good news, and an easy fix. We used a small pair of needle nose pliers to pull out the wire, and patched the tube. As we looked at the other patches and their locations, we concluded that the piece of wire had most likely caused all three holes. We are now hopeful that our flat problems are behind us. We also used a new method to reinstall the tire. We slightly inflated the tube, fitted it into the removed tire, and then carefully installed the tire and tube back onto the rim by hand. We were very satisfied with this repair. Normally you see people leave half of the tire on the rim and just tuck the tube into the tire.

The landscape today was very similar to previous days - not much unusual to see, and very sparsely populated. We did come upon an interesting piece of sculpture. At the top of one of our long climbs, we came upon a large metal piece of artwork in the shape of a bull. I would estimate it to be 20 feet tall. I could actually see it two miles away from another hill.

We continued to struggle against the wind, but after about 30 miles of riding, we rolled into Haskell, Texas. It is a town of about 3,000 residents, and was established before the civil war and named to honor a Texas Revolutionary War hero, Charles Ready Haskell. We decided to eat at a Chinese food restaurant for lunch. The orange chicken was very good, and gave me renewed energy. We also filled our water bottles with ice and water.

As we continued west from Haskell, the wind was starting to shift around to the north. This gave us some relief from the partial headwind that was opposing us before lunch. About 10 miles west of Haskell was the small community of Rule, Texas. We stopped at a convenience store here and filled our water bottles with ice, and then poured a large Gatorade into them over the ice. It was about 85 degrees by then, so we stashed one bottle in our panniers to keep it cold longer. We had about 20 miles left to go, and this was likely our last water stop. Before we left Rule, a gentleman asked us where we were headed and wished us luck after I informed him of our destination. There was also a nice mural on the wall of a downtown building as we left Rule.

From Rule, US 380 turned southwest for a few miles, and with the north wind, we enjoyed a slight push as we pedaled. We made several more rest breaks when we could find a quick stop in the shade and to continue hydrating. One was a roadside picnic area with covered tables, and another was under an abandoned gas station porch at the community of Old Glory. Both provided welcome shade in the breeze. The second water bottle still had ice when we pulled it from our panniers. That is a good trick when it gets hot.

A few other notable items worth mentioning. Many of the fields we passed had cattle or horses, but closer to our destination, we had two horses that ran along the fence keeping up with us for about 1/4 mile. I also noticed several cotton fields that had been harvested. One time today, as we were riding, we noticed a bike tube coiled up like a snake on the side of the shoulder. We decided that we should at least check the size to see if it might useful. I circled back, but it was the wrong valve stem type. At another rest break, we noticed an old concrete boundary line or survey marker. We were always looking for shade for those rest breaks, but the trees were disappearing quickly. The best shade at one stop was a huge light pole near an intersection.

We rolled into the edge of Aspermont and the highway turned north through town. Wow. That north wind hit us in the face at about 25 mph. We were glad it was less than two miles to the motel. At the motel, the clerk must have felt sorry for us, because we were given a room with two beds for the one bed rate.

So, we are now in Aspermont, Texas with over 1,350 miles of riding behind us. We are certainly beyond the halfway point in the journey. Unfortunately, I could not find any church in town with an evening service. I think I would like to make next Sunday a rest day for Easter. I can certainly find a place to worship then.

We are expecting a better day tomorrow - or at least easier. The forecast calls for an east wind, which would be a tailwind. The temperatures should be about 10 degrees cooler, and we are hopeful we will not have to deal with another flat. Our mileage will be about 75 miles to Post, Texas. There are simply not any stops between here and there. Sometimes that is the way it works out.

A large metal bull sculpture on US 380 about 8 to 12 miles west of Throckmorton, TX. It could be seen from far away.

A concrete boundary line or survey marker at one of our rest stops on US 380 near Haskell, TX.

Day 29: March 30, 2015 - Aspermont to Post, TX - 77.2 miles

A Day of (New) Milestones

48 degrees to start, 78 degrees to finish, overcast, 7:30 AM to 6:00 PM, winds E at 5 mph, 10.2 average mph, 26 mph max, 7:30 hours riding time, net elevation change +827 feet. The random mystery word for yesterday was snake.

Verse of the Day: "The urgent request of a righteous person is very powerful in its effect" - James 5:16b

We knew that today would be a long day. There is simply very little between Aspermont and Post, Texas. We began to stir around 6 AM, and walked next door to Hickman's Restaurant for breakfast. I had the breakfast burritos, which were average, but good. After breakfast, we finished packing everything up to head out. We were back on US 380 west just before 7:30 and were blessed to see the sunrise a few minutes down the road. For a while this morning, "Here Comes the Sun" by the Beatles played through my head. It was a chilly but wonderful start to the day.

Bob and I have many discussions during our hours together. We talk about things we remember from childhood, religion, not much politics, dreams, friends, past experiences, and so forth. Bob does more talking than I do; it seems he has an amazing memory. He will remember the name of some person that sold him a shirt at Dillard's 40 years ago. It is uncanny. This morning, the topic was physics. Bob was trying to convince me that we could brainstorm and come up with a perpetual motion machine. He described numerous ways that it might work, but I was skeptical in my responses. I told him we would have to set aside a few laws of physics for his ideas to work. It did pass the time, and that is usually the purpose of much of our chatter.

About 23 miles down the road, we rode into the town of Jayton, Texas. This town of about 500 people was the only place to resupply along our route today. The one place to eat in town was the Boots and Spurs Cafe. I was not even sure that it was open, but we were happy to see an OPEN sign in the window. It was about 10:30, so this would be our second breakfast. We had read of people frequently stopping to eat a second breakfast on these long rides, but this was the first day we had done so.

The cafe was a family owned establishment, and Ishmael waited on us. He was very friendly and enjoyed talking with us, and we with him. He was 20 years old, but had a job offer that he would be able to take when he turned 21. We explained that we would order breakfast, but that we would also order lunch to go. The breakfast was very good, and Ishmael packed up our lunches for the road. If you are biking or driving US 380 near Jayton, I highly recommend this eatery. We also filled our water bottles with ice and water, and we filled a spare bottle before leaving Jayton.

This brings me to one of our milestones. Today we rode 54 miles between services. There was nothing, I mean NOTHING, let me spell it for you, n-o-t-h-i-n-g between Jayton and Post for those 54 miles. Nada. No town, no community, no gas station, no houses close to the road, no water faucets...nothing. We had done our homework, and we knew this would be the case, so we planned accordingly. We simply coped with the situation, as our friend Will had learned to do frequently

The day was long, and we had a few hills. We did not have any flats, and we had a slight tailwind today. It was not so difficult, as it was simply long and tiring. The cloud cover also kept the temperatures down, and that was very nice. As we were getting closer to Post, we had a lady stop and see if we needed anything while we were taking a rest break. That was thoughtful and appreciated. We continue to love US 380 in terms of traffic and drivers. They are all courteous. Traffic was measured by counting the number of minutes between single vehicles.

There were a few more flowers blooming along the route today, but the landscape still was very dry. The few creeks we crossed were nearly dry. We did see a roadrunner and one live rabbit - we had seen several dead ones. We had many views from the tops of ridges today, and I think we could see for 30 miles in many places. I also received a nice follow up email from Planet Bike about the magnet. This is the kind of service you would expect from a small cottage industry, not a larger business.

We are at the Best Western in Post tonight. It is about a mile off of our route, but it works that way from time to time. We had to ride back into town for dinner, which meant that we ate at Dairy Queen again, because it was closer. For other options, we would have to ride 2 miles or more, and we have done enough pedaling for today.

I was glad to see that Bob had an appetite tonight. He has not been eating as much as I have, so I have been concerned about his calorie intake. I told him that many times you have to force yourself to eat when burning the amount of calories that we are burning. Anyway, he ordered the three taco combo with a large drink. Once he polished that off, he went back and ordered a banana pie blizzard, and washed that down with a large order of onion rings. Yes, that was the correct order of things. I think he will be fueled for tomorrow!

Our other milestones were the longest day so far on the trip at 77+ miles, and we also crossed the 1400 total miles threshold. It was also our longest day in terms of time on the bike.

We are tired and ready to rest, but feel that we made a big accomplishment today. Tomorrow looks to be shorter, most likely to Brownfield. We also expect to pick up our package there with our two spare tubes from Randy.

Onward and westward!

Here Comes the Sun! We departed Aspermont, TX, on US 380 early enough to see the sunrise.

One of our rest breaks at a high point on the way to Post, TX, on US 380. We could often see for miles after a climb today.

Day 30: March 31, 2015 - Post to Brownfield, TX - 54.5 miles

Cotton Fields Abound

58 degrees to start, 85 degrees to finish, overcast, 8:30 AM to 4:00 PM, winds SW at 8 mph, 9.2 average mph, 16 mph max, 5:50 hours riding time, net elevation change +705 feet. The random mystery word for yesterday was cottage.

Verse of the Day: "Charm is deceptive and beauty is fleeting, but a woman who fears the LORD will be praised." - Proverbs 31:30

We had a very good breakfast at the Best Western on the north side of Post, Texas this morning. We had our choice of waffles, pancakes, sausage, bacon, eggs, oatmeal, juice, coffee, and more. It was a good start for our ride today. Our distance was less than normal at just over 50 miles, so we waited until 8:30 to leave, allowing us to get a few more minutes of rest.

Just west of Post, again on US 380, we had to climb about 300 feet vertically in about two miles to the top of a plateau in the terrain. From there, it was a slow, steady, gentle climb for most of the day. I will admit the steep climb first thing in the morning was a challenge, but our lowest gears saw us through. A bit more research reveals that we climbed the Caprock Escarpment, a transition from the high level plains to the rolling terrain.

Quite honestly, there is not much out here. We are in west Texas for Pete's sake. The trees are vanishing quickly, and flat land spreads out to the horizon on both sides of the highway. Some fields are growing wild grass and some small shrubs, and other fields are being farmed. A few fields were beginning to be covered in a carpet of small yellow flowers - those were very nice. We saw a lot of cotton fields today. They have all been harvested, and many were being plowed. We saw quite a few tractors at work.

Just before our halfway point today, we rode into Tahoka, Texas. Tahoka is an Indian word meaning 'fresh water'. I do not think that we saw any water out here today, but maybe it was wetter 100 years ago. Our lunch options were limited, so we ended up getting Subway carry out and taking it to a nearby park to eat. We did fill our water bottles, including one with ice and Gatorade which we stashed in our panniers to keep it cold. This method worked well again today, and I still had ice in my water bottle at our last rest stop several hours later.

We continued our push towards Brownfield, fighting some headwind most of the way today. You can tell that the climb and wind lowered our average speed. We did stop at a nice picnic area about 10 miles east of Brownfield for a short rest break. I believe that the area had the most shade and trees that we had seen all day. As we approached Brownfield, we passed about three vineyards beside the highway. Traffic again remained light, and drivers were courteous, including at least one friendly honk. I would also like to note that with the flatness of the terrain, I was able to see Brownfield more than 12 miles before we reached town.

About 20 miles or so before our destination, we began to estimate our arrival time. We also checked the closing time for the Brownfield post office. The package that Randy had sent to Bob (general delivery) had arrived at the post office yesterday. We needed to get there before closing to pick it up. This had our two spare tubes. We did not have any tire issues today, but we were anxious to have spare tubes in our pack again. We picked up the pace for the last couple of hours, utilizing the drafting technique to increase our speed. If you do not know, drafting is where one rider rides very closely behind or slightly to the side of another to reduce wind drag on the rear rider. The method worked well, putting us at the post office with time to spare.

As we approached a stop light in Brownfield, Bob had some trouble dismounting and landed 'gracefully' on the sidewalk. As he was getting back up, I looked back and the lady in the car behind him mouthed "Is he OK?" to me. I gave her a thumbs up, knowing that only his dignity was dented and his nonchalentness was not so nifty. We continued on to the post office, and as we were leaving with our package, we ran into this same woman again. Jeraldyne was an elderly lady and happy to chat. She told us about how friendly her town of Brownfield was. She also elaborated about how her son had done a long bike ride from Lubbock to California some years back. When she told me that she was concerned to see Bob fall back at the light. I told her not to worry, he does it all the time. Well, maybe not all the time, but it has happened on a few occasions. Jeraldyne was a pleasure to meet.

A few blocks north of the post office, we located and checked into the Budget Inn. Budget might be a strong adjective, since we both thought the prices were a bit high for the level of accommodations. Upon entering the office, no one could be found. There was a note on the counter listing a number to call for a manager. This was a strange arrangement, since all of the desk items were not secured and easily within reach including flash drives, the computer, office supplies, etc. We called the number and someone appeared within a minute or so. We were asked questions about whether or not we had pets and if we smoked. To this last question, Bob answered "I don't smoke but I do a lot of drugs". That along with his illegible and cantankerous answers on the registration form led me to believe we might be sleeping on the sidewalk tonight. She took our money anyway.

Looking forward, the next two days look to be hotter with a stronger headwind. A jump to Tatum, New Mexico, (62+ miles) in one shot may be crazy. We have decided to split this into two shorter days, and tackle the headwinds in smaller increments. Tomorrow we would be in Plains, Texas. TripAdvisor does not show any accommodations in Plains. Google shows one motel with a phone number and no more info. I called the number, but did not ever get an answer. This was a problem. So, I looked up the chamber of commerce for Plains. Apparently they do not have a chamber, but the internet search did list a number for the City Hall there. I called City Hall and explained that I was looking for a place to stay. She said there was an inn just north of town. I called the Rock'n N and they do have a room for tomorrow night. The gentleman sounded very friendly and did not even require a credit card to hold it. I will have more details on this tomorrow, but I think it will be a nice change.

We are all set for tonight in Brownfield. Brownfield is a town of about 9,600 residents. The soil in this area is very red due to a high iron content. I was not able to locate any interesting historical facts in my short search this evening.

After showers and a short rest, we walked across the road for dinner. We are looking forward to having two shorter, easier days ahead of us. And, in just two days, we will be out of Texas after a lot of miles in this large state. Happy trails!

Cotton fields east of Tahoka, TX, on US 380. We saw a LOT of cotton fields today, many of them being actively plowed.

Yellow flowers along the side of the road today. We saw many of these patches in fields not being farmed. Between Post and Brownfield, TX, on US 380.

Day 31: April 1, 2015 - Brownfield to Plains, TX - 34.8 miles

We Crossed the 1500 Mile Threshold

60 degrees to start, 78 degrees to finish, sunny, 8:30 AM to 1:30 PM, winds SW at 12 mph, 8.7 average mph, 21 mph max, 4:00 hours riding time, net elevation change +331 feet. The random mystery word for yesterday was computer.

Verse of the Day: "For David says of Him: I saw the Lord ever before me; because He is at my right hand, I will not be shaken." - Acts 2:25

We walked across the street from our motel this morning for another McDonald's big breakfast and OJ. While sitting at the table, Bob pulled the old "your shoe is untied" April fools gag. Real original, Reynolds! I will get him later.

As I said, many times I have a song running through my head. This morning, it was "Give me Jesus, give me Jesus, You can have all this world, But give me Jesus". Great song, performed by various artists.

After breakfast, we walked back to the motel, packed up, and were on the road just after 8:30. This was a good time to depart. We had wanted to be more leisurely with the shorter day, but still were riding before our 9:00 AM plan.

I had one comment posted about the new riding shirt. I really only need one shirt to ride in, since I wash it each night. However, my town shirt, as we call it, was a long sleeve. It is getting warmer, so I wanted a second short sleeve shirt to be able to put on for in town each evening. I went with my bright orange Falls Creek shirt, since I can wear it while riding for good visibility. This color was a stretch for me as an Oklahoma Sooner fan - orange is NOT my color. But, safety first.

As planned, today was to be less than 40 miles. We are once again riding west on US 380, and the southwest and west wind was really starting to kick up. It will be in our face again tomorrow, so trying to cover 60+ miles in one day would have been a killer. We were riding today from Brownfield to Plains, Texas - straight west, with no services in between. Traffic was more than yesterday, but still light to moderate. The headwind really slowed us down today, but we made it to Plains just after lunch time.

As expected, there was not much between towns today. Primarily farm and ranch land, with more fields being plowed for cotton. I did start to see patches of yucca plants, which I had not seen many of before today. I also seemed to notice more oil well pump jacks than on previous days. At one of our rest stops, I told Bob that it looked like he had another flat tire. I was quick to say "April fools" before he passed out and fell to the concrete. I don't think he wanted to fix another flat tire today. We have not had any more tire issues since removing that tiny piece of wire a few days back. We talked about several topics to pass the time... childhood friends, old jokes and tricks in school, but not much finance like yesterday.

Plains, Texas, is a town of about 1,500 people, and it is the westernmost town on US 380 in Texas. Most incomes in this area are based upon agriculture and the oil industry.

I let Bob pick lunch as we rolled into town, so we ended up at Dairy Queen. He sure seems to like that place. I went with the crispy chicken salad - I really am trying to avoid eating all junk food. As we were finishing our Blizzards (ok, some junk food), a lady walked up to our table and said, "Are you guys supposed to be eating ice cream?" To which I replied, "As far as we are riding, we can eat anything we want." As expected, she was one of the owners of the B&B we reserved for tonight. Janice Newsom introduced herself and said that when she saw the bikes outside, she figured we were her guests. I had told her husband yesterday evening that we were on bicycles.

Janice was nice enough to give us a ride to the grocery store in town, where we purchased items so that we can make dinner at the B&B tonight. She then dropped us back at our bikes, and she drove our groceries on to the guest house. They do not live on the property, but it does have a full kitchen. We really appreciated her hospitality. The house also has a washer and dryer, so we will wash all of our clothes tonight. Since the property is about 2.5 miles from town, we do not plan to leave again until we head out for breakfast in the morning. Their other guests do not need breakfast, so we got a price break for the room only. If you are bicycling US 380, and are anywhere near Plains, Texas, I highly recommend you consider staying at the Rock'n-N Bed and Breakfast. Contact Janice or Neal Newsom via their website at www.newsomvineyards.com or call 806-456-7885.

Another interesting bit of news from home... Jana emailed me to let me know that this grand adventure got mentioned in the Murray State College Alumni & Friends newsletter. You can check it out here: http://www.mscok.edu/sites/www/Uploads/files/AlumniFriends/Alumni%20 Newsletter%20Sp2015.pdf

We have rolled beyond the 1,500 mile point today. Bob stopped to take pictures. He told me that mentally, that was his "point of no return". We have right at 60%

of the miles behind us, and we think that we have less than 1,000 miles to go from here.

We cooked dinner tonight in the house, and we really enjoyed visiting with Neal and two other guests staying here, Brock and Larry. The cool Texas evening on the back porch was wonderful.

Neal has offered to drive us and our bikes back into town tomorrow morning before 7:00 for breakfast at Amigo's. The Newsom's hospitality has been fantastic. We can't thank you enough. Now, if I can just get this posted along with some photos and then get to sleep!

Things are beginning to green up in some places. East of Plains, TX, on US 380.

A nice welcome sign for Plains, TX, on US 380.

New Mexico

Day 32: April 2, 2015 - Plains, TX to Tatum, NM - 33.1 miles

New Mexico - State # 7 & Mountain Time

47 degrees to start, 75 degrees to finish, sunny, 7:30 AM to 12:30 PM, winds SW at 10 mph, 8.9 average mph, 13 mph max, 3:40 hours riding time, net elevation change +358 feet. The random mystery word for yesterday was finance.

Verse of the Day: "For the LORD gives wisdom, and from his mouth come knowledge and understanding." - Proverbs 2:6

We were up early today. Neal, the B&B owner, arrived just after 6:30 AM when it was still dark. We loaded our bikes into his truck, and he gave us a ride back to town. We had already ridden those miles, so we did not feel obligated to ride them again. Neal joined us for breakfast at Amigo's. I had the ham and sausage breakfast burrito that included cheese and potatoes. Bob went more American with oatmeal, two eggs, and toast with the crust removed. The restaurant had the Lubbock news on the television, and they announced that pastor Jon Randles passed away last night. Jana and I had heard him speak at several revivals and marriage conferences. He was a faithful preacher.

After breakfast, we again were headed west on US 380 out of Plains, Texas. The sun was just about to break above the horizon as we left town. It may only be 30 miles or so, but there was nothing between Plains and Tatum, New Mexico. Very little of the land was being farmed, but it may have been ranch land. With the drought, there is likely not enough vegetation for cattle at this time.

About 15 miles west of Plains, we crossed from Texas into New Mexico. We were disappointed with the lack of any real welcome sign for New Mexico. We also crossed into Mountain Time at this line. Traffic was again light on US 380 today. The southwest winds were starting to pick up, but it was still tolerable in the morning hours. We also saw one jack rabbit at one of our rest stops. Our last stop was at the only picnic area on this section of highway, about 5 miles east of Tatum.

We were soon rolling into Tatum, New Mexico. Signs told us that the elevation was 4,100 feet here. Tatum is a town of about 650 people, founded in 1909. There is some sort of metal sign and art company in town, because metal signs and art are everywhere. They are made into street signs, business signs, ranch gate signs, and so forth. You may see some of them in the pictures.

Near the middle of town, after the only stop light, we pulled into Tiny's Burger Barn for lunch. We found out that Tiny no longer owns the restaurant. We enjoyed a couple of burger baskets and relaxed for a few minutes. We also chatted with a gentleman wearing an OU cap. He said he had family in Oklahoma. He told us if we came by his place one mile south of town, he would show us around his property. We thanked him for the offer, but that was the wrong direction for us.

We asked the hostess if she knew anything about the Sunset Inn motel at the west edge of town. We had tried to call several times, but did not ever get an answer. The hostess said that she thought it was open, and the owner eats there from time to time. We decided to ride the mile and a half west to check it out.

Upon arriving at the Sunset Inn motel, it appeared that the sun had indeed set on this motel. The office was locked, and no one was home. There were two dogs inside that made it clear they did not like us. Bob walked around and most of the room doors were unlocked. Many were trashed, or used for storage or perhaps beer parties. One room that had beds did not have working electricity or water. We discussed our options. Should we wait for someone or try something else? I did not think there were any other motels in town.

We decided to call city hall to find out what they might know. The person who answered the phone 'thought' the motel was open, but he also said there was another option, the Sands Motel. I called the number provided, and a gentleman answered and told me that he had one room with two beds for $50. We really did not have any other options, since Roswell was 70+ miles west into a headwind that was increasing by the minute.

We rode the mile or so back into town and found the Sands on the south side of the highway. The 'lobby' was furnished with 1950s worn out sofas, numerous ashtrays full of butts, and reeked of smoke. He told a lady to go get our room ready, and said it would only be a minute. I struggled to breathe while we paid our fee and were given a key.

We headed to the room here at the Bates motel - seriously, it is the worst place I have ever stayed. The carpet is 35 years old and filthy. They told us the bed has clean sheets, so that is good. The door jamb does not have any trim, so we can see outside through the gap. The walls are dirty, and the shower has some sort of black growth not seen since my college dorm room days. I knew my Xero ultralight sandals would come in handy - a great barrier between my feet and germ central. All is not lost, we do have a microwave, fridge, and Wi-Fi. And, the bed will be better than sleeping outside on the ground, I think. I wrote this feeling quite confident that no one in town knows about this journal, and will not find it until we are long gone. I just want to warn future cyclists what they may be getting into here in Tatum. It is not that I feel unsafe, just unclean. Oh well, we will cope and I am sure there are worse places to be in for one night. I will say that they have good towels, which smelled strongly of bleach, so I am hopeful all germs are dead on their linens. Also, the owner of the Sands, a friendly guy originally from Hugo, Oklahoma, said there was some big drug bust at the Sunset Inn and that it is likely closed due to that issue.

We are back from dinner. I think there are three places to eat in town, so we have now been to two of them. The Steakhouse Cafe is famous for their real steak fingers. I must admit, they were good - but so was the salad, roll, and pecan pie with ice cream. A guy's got to eat, you know. On the way to dinner, we met Joel, who was doing a bike tour around New Mexico. I think he needs to use more sunscreen. He was from Michigan, and rode in from Roswell with the tailwind today.

We are back at the room to finish up our journals. We also need to do a few minor bike maintenance items - seat treatment, tire pressure, and adjust Bob's rear shifter. Also, Bob's friend Del is supposed to arrive tonight. He will ride one day with us tomorrow.

The plan for tomorrow is to make the run to Roswell. This is a famous stretch for turning back riders for multiple days. For instance, riding back from dinner tonight, we had to battle 25 to 30 mph headwinds from the southwest. That would make the ride to Roswell from here, with no places to stop in between, nearly impossible. We are extremely thankful for what looks to be a great forecast for tomorrow. The high is supposed to be about 65 degrees. But, more importantly, the wind is predicted to switch around to the north and then northeast during the day tomorrow. This will be a cross wind, but not a headwind, for the 72 miles we will have to cover tomorrow.

This is the only welcome sign as we entered New Mexico on US 380. Sad. But, this meant that we have entered state # 7 today.

A nice metal work display in Tatum, NM, on US 380. All of those flags and images are done in metal.

Day 33: April 3, 2015 - Tatum to Roswell, NM - 74.4 miles

A Visitor Joins Us

42 degrees to start, 68 degrees to finish, sunny, 7:45 AM to 4:00 PM, winds NE at 20 mph then diminishing, 12.5 average mph, 39 mph max, 6:00 hours riding time, net elevation change -423 feet. The random mystery word for yesterday was crust (Bob hid his word in a typo).

Verse of the Day: "Honor the Lord with your possessions and with the first produce of your entire harvest" - Proverbs 3:9

We needed to make sure that we had time today in the daylight to get to Roswell, so we left the motel at 6:30 to go eat breakfast. Del was with us for today's ride, so we took his car to the Steakhouse Cafe. They make a good breakfast as well as dinner. I enjoyed pancakes, ham, hash browns, eggs (over medium), grapefruit juice, and coffee. A full stomach is a great way to start the daily ride. After breakfast we drove back to the motel to get our bikes ready to leave. I will also mention that although our room at the Sand's Motel was terrible, the room that Del and his wife Jo had, was rustic, but remodeled. If you come through, you might look at the room before you pay for it.

First of all, it was cold this morning. My bike computer registered 42 degrees as we headed west out of Tatum. The wind was howling out of the north or northeast at 20 to 25 mph. I did not calculate the wind chill, but I am sure that it was quite low.

Since Del was biking with us today, his wife Jo carried food for lunch and extra water in the car. There is not a single gas station between Tatum and Roswell.

The first 25 or so miles out of Tatum were west and northwest, doing a slow climb, much like the last couple of days. This put us in a stiff cross wind, but at least it was not a head wind. We stopped at a small store at Caprock, but it was closed and no one was home. I am glad that we did not depend on it for a resupply point.

There was very little to see on this segment today. Almost no trees, wide open spaces, no farming, a few cattle, and many tumbleweeds. I did see a herd of sheep on the south side of the road at one point, and then they all starting running as we approached.

At about 31 miles into the day, the road turned back straight west, which provided more of a tailwind. There was one picnic area, with restrooms, in fact. Jo met us there with the car, and we had a picnic lunch. The wind made it tough to hold on to your plate, but we appreciated her providing us with sandwiches, chips, pretzels, fresh fruit, and Gatorade. We refilled our water bottles at this stop.

From this point on the route, US 380 started a slow descent towards Roswell. There were still a few climbs, and we enjoyed a few steep downhills, but in general the decline just made pedaling easier. The wind began to subside, but we still had a decent tailwind heading toward Roswell, New Mexico.

We took a few breaks along the way, but our speed increased with the slope and wind. It also warmed up as the day progressed, so we shed several layers as time went by.

Del did great, and the three of us made good time to Roswell. Traffic was more moderate on the highway today, but drivers gave us plenty of room. We did not have any problems, and several vehicles honked or waved. We did pass a couple of historical markers. And we crossed the Pecos River east of Roswell. That was the only water that we saw today.

We pedaled all the way across town to check in at the Rodeway Inn. The motel looks good, and the price was right. I asked if we could get a ground floor room, since we were on bicycles. They told us we could, for $9 more. We declined. We have ridden over 1600 miles, and spent 32+ nights on the road, and this is the first place that has made us carry the bicycles up the stairs to an upper room. Every other place of lodging has had an elevator, or given us a first floor room at the same price.

After cleaning up, Del and his wife took us out to eat. We enjoyed Mexican food at Tia Juana's in Roswell. Thanks! We then stopped by the grocery store to buy food for lunch tomorrow. I do not think that we have many options as we start the climb up into the mountains. Del seems to be a glutton for punishment, and wants to ride until lunch with us tomorrow. We welcome the company and having Jo meet us with lunch supplies again will be appreciated.

I also got a few texts from Doug, the Scoutmaster of the Boy Scout troop that he and I work with. They are camping at his place this weekend, and all the guys said hello. Dr. Reel has graciously taken my place on the camp out since I am on this grand adventure.

Well, it was a good day. A bitter start, but a nice finish. Lots more miles are behind us now. The good food and good company were enjoyable. But, we need to start early again to take advantage of the daylight. Goodnight all.

Move along, nothing to see here.... Our view of the barren landscape - this was what we viewed all day. Sometimes it is like that. Between Roswell and Tatum, NM, on US 380.

We crossed the Pecos River just east of Roswell, on US 380.

Day 34: April 4, 2015 - Roswell to Lincoln, NM - 54.4 miles

Our Biggest Climb

48 degrees to start, 66 degrees to finish, overcast, 7:45 AM to 3:45 PM, winds SE at 10 mph, 9.4 average mph, 31 mph max, 5:45 hours riding time, net elevation change +2156 feet. The random mystery word for yesterday was stomach.

Verse of the Day: "Carefully consider the path for your feet, and all your ways will be established." - Proverbs 4:26

Today was the day we began to climb into the mountains. The total of all climbs today was 2700 feet, with a net elevation gain of 2100 feet. This will likely be the largest net elevation gain for any one day of our trip. I was concerned about the difficulty of the day, to be honest.

Del was returning home today, but decided to ride until lunch with us. That would give him a personal two day best total distance of over 100 miles. This also had the advantage for us of his wife Jo being able to carry lunch in the car and meet us at about noon today.

We ate the motel breakfast. They advertised a 'full hot breakfast', but I think they need to look around at their competition. It was about half of what other good motels have done. We ate the best breakfast that we could, and were ready to roll out at 7:45 this morning.

The elevation profile showed a steady gain all morning, then a short drop about half way, followed by a steady gain into Lincoln. We had a south or southwest wind, providing a partial tailwind at times. The shoulders on US 380 leaving Roswell were quite good. The highway was four lane and divided, and that worked really well for us. It was cold, but not as cold as yesterday.

We had one steep climb at about mile 24, which was challenging. The rest of the day was mostly steady climbs, and then a short steep descent, before climbing again. The tail wind did help, but it was not nearly as steep of a climb as I was expecting.

The landscape began to change, and that was a welcome sight. We got our first glimpse of the southern Rockies, and the rolling terrain was much more interesting. We still did not see many trees, and the climate is dry, but at least it is not so flat that we can see 20 miles in every direction.

At one of our rest stops, just before a large drop in elevation, we saw another loaded bike tourer. He did not stop, since the highway was divided, but he was loaded down. I would estimate 60 to 100 pounds of gear in the front and rear sets of panniers. After we have been traveling so light, I cannot imagine how someone would want to carry that much gear. To each his own, I guess.

At around mile 33, Jo met us with the car for lunch. We made peanut butter and jelly sandwiches, and ate fruit and bananas. I made up the rest of the bread into sandwiches and we packed it in our panniers for later. We are not expecting to find any place to eat dinner in Lincoln tonight.

We have enjoyed having Del with us, and he and Jo were very generous, loading us up with protein bars, Gatorade, and other items to have as backup food supplies. They are heading home today, so we parted company after lunch.

After lunch, we rode northwest on US 380 / US 70 through the small communities of Picacho, Tinne, and Hondo. The only gas station on the route today was in Hondo, so we stopped for a few snacks. Just after Hondo, US 70 splits and goes more west, while US 380 narrows to two lane and becomes the Billy the Kid Highway towards Lincoln.

The two lane road did not have a shoulder, but it did not bother us since traffic had also become extremely light. About 10 miles up the valley on Billy the Kid

Highway, we came to the town of Lincoln, New Mexico. The town has quite a storied history, but I am not able to get online right now to find out anything in detail about it. We have been following a river up a valley for the last 20 miles or so.

Near the south edge of town, we came upon the Ellis Country Store and Inn. This old establishment advertises that Billy the Kid actually slept there. We had reserved a room, and David greeted us as we arrived. This inn has history and charm throughout. It should be an enjoyable stay, with a cooked to order full breakfast provided in the morning.

The room is rustic, and filled with antiques. The old walls are about 12 inches thick, and winter heating is provided by an old wood burning stove with a metal stove pipe chimney.

Tomorrow is Easter, and we are headed to church. The closest town with a church is Capitan, 12 miles up the road. We expect that we can easily ride that short distance after our good breakfast in the morning. There are three churches there, and at least one listed an 11 AM service on their website. I am looking forward to worship tomorrow.

I went down to the living area to write or read. Another family (Bill, Paula, and kids) was staying here, and we talked about our trip and learned about each other. They are not blood relatives, but like family to the Inn owners, Dave and Jinny. No one else is here this weekend, so Jinny asked if we wanted to join them for dinner. Jinny at one point was recognized as the best chef in New Mexico. What a dinner! She 'just threw together' lasagna, fresh salad, Italian bread, bread pudding, cheese cake, and crème brûlée. We dined by candle light while listening to Frank Sinatra music. It was a very nice time. We expected to eat PB&J in our room, so this was quite a surprise.

They have invited us to all ride by car with them to Capitan for church tomorrow, and then we will return for breakfast. We are overwhelmed by their kindness and inclusiveness.

Our first glimpse of the southern end of the Rockies. Between Roswell and Lincoln, NM, on US 380.

Riding up the valley on US 380 (Billy the Kid Trail) between Honda and Lincoln, NM. We follow the Bonito River as we travel up the valley.

Day 35: April 5, 2015 - Lincoln to Carrizozo, NM - 32.8 miles

Easter Sunday

60 degrees to start, 68 degrees to finish, sunny, 11:30 AM to 5:00 PM, winds SW at 15 to 25 mph, 7.4 average mph, 27 mph max, 4:20 hours riding time, net elevation change -286 feet. The random mystery word for yesterday was chimney.

Verse of the Day: "He has been resurrected! He is not here!" - Mark 16:6 (partial, used in the sermon this morning)

The innkeepers, Dave and Jinny, had invited us to attend church with them this morning in Capitan. We loaded up in vehicles at 8:00 for the short drive up the highway. We attended the Easter service at the Sacred Heart Catholic Church in Capitan, New Mexico. It was a different worship experience for me, but it was also interesting. You see, my worship does not depend on the building, the surroundings, or the type of music. Worship is between me and my God, and in that I was successful today.

After church, we returned to the Inn. Bob and I began to pack, while Dave, Jinny, Bill, and Kathy started on breakfast. We soon joined them in the kitchen, but there was not a lot that we could do. They had things running quite smoothly. We all sat down for a family style breakfast of eggs, bacon, toast, hash browns, and fresh fruit. It was all delicious. We soon had to say our goodbyes. We very much appreciated Dave and Jinny's hospitality.

We decided to ride the 30 or so miles to Carrizozo. The route appeared to climb to Capitan, and then be a good downhill. We expected a short, easy ride. However, once we reached Capitan, the wind was really starting to pick up. We also still had several more miles to climb before reaching Indian Divide at 6,952 feet. So, we started this morning in Lincoln (about 5,700 ft), rode through Capitan (6,530 ft) over Indian Divide and down to Carrizozo (5,429 ft). Our easy day turned into more work than I expected. I felt bad that it was not an easier day for Bob.

The ride had good scenery. We had many nice views, but it was sometimes hard to look around with the wind battering us. We had to focus on keeping the bike rolling straight. We did not see many houses or structures between towns. I saw one house with a lot of metal work, including white metal bars on all of the doors and windows to keep out a thief.

We passed one other bicycle tourer. William was headed east. He had left San Diego about two weeks ago. He is headed to Key West, but plans to wander a bit on the way. It was nice to see another bicyclist on this route.

Tomorrow we are heading to Socorro. The problem is that once we leave Carrizozo, we will not have any services for 60 miles. We will need to pack plenty of water and our lunch. We are hoping the winds will not be as strong tomorrow.

US 380 or Billy the Kid Trail between Lincoln and Capitan.
Nice scenery.

Heading down toward Carrizozo. I don't think I pedaled for two miles through here. On US 380 east of Carrizozo, NM - east of Indian Divide.

Day 36: April 6, 2015 - Carrizozo, New Mexico - 0 miles

Rest Day - Valley of Fires

The secret mystery word for yesterday was: thief.

Verse of the Day: "We look not at the things which are seen, but at the things which are not seen, for the things which are seen are temporal, but the things which are not seen are eternal." – 2 Corinthians 4:18 (one of the quoted passages in Pilgrim's Progress, which I began reading today.)

Bob did not sleep last night and needed a rest day, so we stayed put in Carrizozo.

I got out and about to see what I could find that was interesting. Being Monday, many things were closed, but I still managed to find a few intriguing points of interest.

First, I headed across the street to Abuelita's Restaurant for a green chili omelet. That got the sinuses opened up! I then walked over to the Visitor's Center. The chamber of commerce and visitor information are housed in an old caboose. They were closed, but I did read some information about the town near the caboose.

As I was about to walk back to the motel, two bicycle tourers rode up to also see what was at the Visitor's Center. I walked over and introduced myself and asked where they were headed. Julia and Gina are from Germany. They had been in Los Angeles working as translators, but they decided to bicycle to Chicago. They were loaded down, lots of bags and things strapped on. They are primarily camping, and they are headed to Fort Worth to see some friends on the way. I told them about our route and recommended US 380, since it had been a good road for us. I told them some information about our trip and where we were headed. I wished them luck and walked back to the motel.

Back at the room, we decided to eat lunch around 2 PM to give Bob more resting time. So, I was in need of something to keep me busy until our late lunch. My daughter Micah says I have to be doing something, and maybe that is true. Those words of Longfellow resonate well with me: "Let us then be up and doing, with a heart for any fate, still achieving, still pursuing, learn to labor, and to wait." So, while I waited on Bob to rest, I was off to pursue something of interest in the area.

I had seen signs for the Valley of Fires Recreation Area about 4 miles from town. I decided to take the bike and head that way. It was windy, but the terrain was flat. The recreation area is adjacent to a 44 mile long lava flow from Little Black Peak, and the flow varies from four to six miles wide in the Tularosa Basin. The visitor center was closed, but there were campsites and a nature walking trail. There were two or three RVs in the area. The nature trail was very well built and maintained, with signs describing the landscape, as well as plant and animal life. It was amazing to see the number of plants growing among the lava flow - quite a picture of God's handiwork for sure. I walked around the nature trail, enjoyed the scenery, and took several photos.

As I was coming back up the nature trail entrance, I met two gentlemen that asked me about the bike - I had locked it at the top of the trail. They were also cyclists, though not tourers. We chatted for a few minutes about our trip and the area. They warned me of the goat heads.

After visiting the Valley of Fires, I rode back to town and around some of the streets to see what was located here. It is a small town of less than 1,000. Soon, I headed back to the motel to meet up with Bob for lunch, but I did manage to put 11.5 miles on the bike (not counted toward the trip total) with my sightseeing. I think Bob might have gotten too cold this morning, because I noticed the thermostat was off on the air conditioner. Those units can be finicky at times.

For lunch, we went back to Abuelita's, since it was so close to our motel. The cheeseburger and fries were quite good.

We will eat dinner later, pack up supplies for tomorrow's lunch, and get to bed early to be ready for the ride to Socorro. We will try to leave early to get up and over the next pass before the winds kick up. That's life in the mountains.

Julie and Gina, bicycle tourers that started in LA. They are from Germany originally, headed to Chicago. They were loaded, but appeared to be making progress. We met at the Carrizozo, NM, visitor center. Guten Tag!

A view across the lava field at the Valley of Fires just west of Carrizozo, NM, on US 380.

Day 37: April 7, 2015 - Carrizozo to Socorro, NM - 74.5 miles

Big Climb, Big Miles

50 degrees to start, 78 degrees to finish, sunny, 7:00 AM to 6:00 PM, winds SW at 10 to 25 mph, 9.5 average mph, 30 mph max, 7:50 hours riding time, net elevation change -833 feet. The random mystery word for yesterday was thermostat.

Verse of the Day: "...For I assure you: If you have faith the size of a mustard seed, you will tell this mountain, 'Move from here to there,' and it will move. Nothing will be impossible for you." - Matthew 17:20 (I cannot imagine why I thought of this passage while spending four hours climbing mountains today ;-)

We were up at 6:00 this morning, planning for a 7:00 AM departure from Carrizozo. We wanted to do as much climbing as possible before the afternoon winds became gusty.

We headed west out of town on US 380 again. This would be our final day on a highway that we have become very familiar with. We first joined US 380 way back in east Texas, in Greenville. With the exception of McKinney to Denton, the road has been good, shoulders have been adequate, and traffic has been moderate to light to non-existent.

The first few miles today descended slightly as we headed mostly northwest. About 4 miles out of town, we passed the entrance to the Valley of Fires recreation area. I highly recommend a visit to this lava flow. We rode through the lava flow area for 3 or 4 miles this morning.

Soon after, we began climbing. We would have two climbs today. One shorter climb early over a smaller ridge, followed by a short descent, and then a long, prolonged climb over the mountain range. The short climb was not too bad. We kept our bikes in lower gears and kept our feet spinning. One advantage of a touring bike is the low range of gears. We can be down in the lowest gear and do 3 or 4 mph up a mountain.

The second climb was long, as in hours long. It had steep sections at times, but it was mostly the length that was challenging. It was nearly 26 miles from Carrizozo to where we finally made the pass and finished our major climb for the day.

Since this had taken us about 4 hours, we went ahead and took a break for lunch. We had previously purchased all of the ingredients for peanut butter and jelly, so we made a few sandwiches and fueled back up for the rest of the day. We still had about 50 miles to go!

The west side of the mountain was really nice. We rode about 4 miles down with very little pedaling. I was running 25 to 30 mph, coasting, for nearly 2 miles. At about 4 miles after the summit, we pulled into a roadside picnic area for a quick break. As I rode in, I realized that there was another bicycle tourer parked at a picnic table.

Rob was 57 and heading to North Carolina. He had done a long tour last year, and he was doing another long ride again this year. He was quite loaded with front bags, rear bags, a trunk bag, and then a cardboard box on top of that. He seemed to be in shape for it, telling me that he was riding about 80 miles a day on average. We chatted for a few minutes, and then parted ways, both needing to put more miles behind us.

Our decline soon flattened out, and we were riding in the valley on our way to San Antonio, just south of Socorro. We could see the mountains on the other side of Socorro, which were about 35 miles away. We watched those mountains for hours today, and it seemed like we would never get to them.

There was very little between Carrizozo and San Antonio, maybe one or two houses and a rock shop that was closed. No services, no gas stations, no water.

We had filled about three extra water bottles, in addition to the two bottles on each bike, just to be sure that we had enough drinking water today.

About ten miles east of San Antonio, we were surprised to see a few more descents towards the Rio Grande. We could see the green valley below, where they were likely irrigating along the river. These drops in elevation gave us some rest and increased our speed.

Just before San Antonio, we crossed the Rio Grande and stopped for a few photos. This was the most water we had seen in many days. The river was muddy, but quite full.

We had a recommendation to stop at the Owl Bar & Grill for a burger if we passed that way. It turns out that the establishment was right on our route, at the turn off of US 380 onto NM Route 1.

As we walked in, Don greeted us. He was a patron, but had seen us ride up on the bikes. He asked the usual questions, but was stunned to hear that we were headed to Ocean Beach. He had lived in Ocean Beach for many years.

We ordered our food (I had a green chili cheeseburger), and continued to visit with Don and his wife. They owned the rock shop that we had seen about 30 miles back on our route. Don asked why and how we were undertaking the trip. Bob explained that I had retired and joined him on this adventure. Don asked his wife why she was not retired yet, and she said that it was likely due to the fact that she previously liked to party too much. Interesting folks. They said that they have seen many bicyclists pass through from time to time.

The early dinner was tasty and energizing, but we still had about ten miles to go. We headed north on NM 1, basically running parallel to I-25. We entered Socorro from the south, and since we would be taking US 60 tomorrow, we found a motel on the south end of town. The location will work well for our departure towards Magdalena in the morning.

Here are a few interesting facts about our day. Our starting elevation in Carrizozo was 5,425 feet. Our highest elevation coming over the mountains today was about 6,600 feet. The elevation here at Socorro is 4,603 feet. Debris on the shoulder included a very clean paintbrush, scissors, and a smashed RV sewer hose.

Until tomorrow...

It is all downhill (mostly) from here. Taken at the top of our climb at around 6,600 feet between Carrizozo and San Antonio, NM, on US 380.

Crossing the Rio Grande, just east of San Antonio, NM, on US 380. We had not seen this much water in some time.

Day 38: April 8, 2015 - Socorro to Magdalena, NM - 26.5 miles

Happy Birthday to the One I Love

55 degrees to start, 68 degrees to finish, sunny, 8:00 AM to 1:00 PM, winds SW at 15 to 30 mph, 7.1 average mph, 20 mph max, 3:45 hours riding time, net elevation change +1972 feet. The random mystery word for yesterday was party.

Verse of the Day: "For wisdom is better than jewels, and nothing desirable can compare with it." - Proverbs 8:11

Today was a short day, mostly because tomorrow is forced to be a long day by our lodging options. It worked out well, because we had a big climb again today, but with much worse winds.

From Socorro, we started a gradual ascent, but then began a long, big climb for a total of 10 miles. The winds were starting to whip up this morning, and the cross winds nearly blew me off the road at several times on the climb. I had one tumbleweed that I could not avoid get stuck in my front fender, so I had to stop and remove it.

I do not know how to adequately describe it, but we were pedaling up very steep mountains, while being blown from the side by 15 to 25 mph cross winds. I think some of the climbs were so steep we could have used a ladder! It was a slow arduous process, and it was a full 10 miles before we reached the top of the plateau.

Once the task of climbing was complete, we turned to head northwest. We actually had a tail wind on the flat for several miles, but as the highway turned back to the southwest, the wind was in our face again. The last 8 miles or so were a less steep climb to Magdalena, but we had the 25 to 35 mph gusty winds in our face. It was extremely slow going, often pedaling 4 or 5 mph.

We started at Socorro at an elevation of around 4,600 feet and ended at Magdalena at an elevation of about 6,500 feet.

Once we finally made it to Magdalena, we were in search of a restaurant for a much needed lunch. I spotted a cafe sign, so we turned and went one block off of US 60 to the MM Cafe. They offered some homemade wholesome items with fresh ingredients. The roast beef and provolone was very good, as was the bean soup with bacon.

As we were talking with Linda (I think she runs the place), she asked where we were staying. I told her where we planned to stay, but that we had not paid for anything yet. She was happy to show me a room in the old hotel building, the same building that housed the cafe. The rate was very reasonable and the room was quite large. It was nice to not have to go back out in search of another place in town to stay. As an added bonus, the cafe serves dinner until 7:00 tonight, with several homemade dishes on the menu. Thank you Linda! After a hearty lunch, we went to the room to shower and rest.

Magdalena is a town of about 900 and is trying to draw tourism through art and culture. The town was once a mining boom town after the Kelly Mine opened, only a few miles from town. Cibola National Forest land is north and south of Magdalena.

Since we had extra time this afternoon, we went back to the MM Cafe after some rest and had smoothies. The Berry Frontier was delicious.

We are now back from dinner, where we loaded up on fantastic chicken alfredo. That should serve us well tomorrow on the ride to Quemado. Oh, we also surpassed 1800 miles today, so that is a nice milestone.

At the top of our steep and windy climb just west of Socorro on our way to Magdalena, NM, on US 60. We climbed about 2,000 vertical feet over approximately 10 miles.

Chicken alfredo at the MM Cafe, included a fresh salad, and all for $8. I definitely recommend them in Magdalena on US 60.

Day 39: April 9, 2015 - Magdalena to Quemado, NM - 79.0 miles

We Crossed the Continental Divide

34 degrees to start, 68 degrees to finish, sunny, 8:00 AM to 6:30 PM, winds variable at 5 mph, 10.0 average mph, 33 mph max, 7:50 hours riding time, net elevation change +315 feet. The random mystery word for yesterday was ladder.

Verse of the Day: "The fear of the Lord is the beginning of wisdom, and the knowledge of the Holy One is understanding." - Proverbs 9:10

Since it was going to be quite cold this morning, we delayed our riding start time until about 8:00 AM. We left the hotel and rode a couple of blocks to the Magdalena Cafe for breakfast. It was quite good, and just what I needed to get the day started.

As we left Magdalena on US 60 heading west, we had a long gradual climb for about 10 miles. At times it was hard to know for sure that we were climbing, but our speed will always tell the story. After this climb, we dropped down slightly into a wide flat valley. When I say wide, I mean we could see the straight road out in front of us for 20 miles!

As I started today, I was reminded of one of my favorite quotes. This one is by John Muir... "The mountains are calling, and I must go..." This was a fitting thought for today, considering the heights we would by cycling over, and the great mountain scenery that would soon surround us.

On the way up the first climb, we stopped at a picnic area. There was a historical marker telling some history of the Magdalena Livestock Driveway. This cattle and sheep drive route was used all the way up until 1971.

Soon, we were over that first climb and dropping down slightly to the wide valley below. This was part of the plains of San Augustin. This is also where the VLA or Very Large Array astronomical radio observatory is located. It consists of 27 dish antennas, each 82 feet in diameter. We could see it for miles, but it seemed to take forever to finally reach it on this long straight section of US 60.

The VLA did have a visitor center, but it was 4 miles off the highway. This is an inconsequential distance in a gasoline powered hulk of steel, but for our human powered machines, it was a bit too far away. We did stop at the rest site near the closest VLA antennas, but they did not have a picnic table or even a sign telling about the VLA. This will be a good place to visit in the future.

At about mile 35 today, we entered the small community of Datil. It was at the far side of the plain, just as we started to climb into more mountains. The only business we were interested in at Datil was the Eagle Ranch Cafe. This was almost half way for our day, and we were ready to eat. The Eagle Ranch has been in existence for many years, and has only been owned by three different families. We had a couple of very good sandwiches.

While we were seated for lunch, a very friendly lady came over to ask us about our trip. Nita, who runs a hostel in Pie Town for hikers on the Continental Divide Trail (CDT), also hosts bicyclists from time to time. We commented to her that we were quite sad that Pie Town does not have any places that serve pie on Thursdays in April. (Yes, this seemed odd to us as well.) Nita informed us that there was a new place, and they were open today. We were very excited to learn that we might indeed have some pie in Pie Town today. She said that the new pie shop would be open today until they sold out of pie. We paid our lunch bill, skipped any dessert, and headed out towards Pie Town.

Two milestones for the day would occur before we reached Pie Town, New Mexico. First, we would hit our highest elevation to date on the trip, which was right around 8,100 feet. Second, we would cross the continental divide, which due to topography, was not the highest point of our ride today. Think about it a while, and it might confuse you.

Another song got stuck in my brain as we pedaled along today. This one is by John Fogerty titled "Proud Mary". I am sure you know it, the lyrics in my head today were:

> Bike wheels keep on turnin'
> Strong legs keep on churnin'
> Rollin'... Rollin'... Rollin' down the asphalt

Our climb from Datil to the high point for the day was gradual and not too steep, certainly nothing like yesterday's vertical ascent. We have been climbing hills for so long that up looks flat and flat looks down. A few miles after the maximum elevation for the day, we crossed the Continental Divide, elevation 7,786. This is a major milestone on our trip, much like crossing the Mississippi River several weeks ago. It is certainly not all downhill from here, but we are making great progress.

Just a couple of miles after the divide, we rolled into Pie Town. This town has three or four cafes that serve, among other things, pie. Most are closed Thursday, but we were hopeful that Nita's suggestion would lead us to a tasty slice of pie. As we approached the driveway and saw the sign for The Pie Source, our hearts sank. The gate was locked, they must have sold out of pie for the day. Honestly, how can a town called Pie Town, not have enough pie for everyone that might want some on any day of the year?

We rode a few hundred more yards into town and stopped at Pie-O-Neer pies. This is one of the most famous establishments, and we knew they would be closed. As we were taking a few photos, a lady came from around back and told us that if we rode down to the next intersection, and turned left, we would find the Toaster House Hostel. She was sure that they would have some pie in the freezer for the CDT hikers. What joy filled our minds! We had another chance for some Pie Town pie.

So, back on the bikes, down the hill, we turned onto a gravel road (we hate these), and rode back up another hill (also not our favorite thing), and we found the Toaster House Hostel. It is called the Toaster House because affixed to the fence posts in the front yard are old electric toasters. There were several CDT hikers hanging out on the porch. We introduced ourselves and told them we came in search of pie. They informed us that Nita had been feeding it to them, and they were not sure there was any left. We walked around to the back porch and checked the freezer - it had frozen pizza, but not pie. Our hopes were dashed again.

We chatted with the hikers for several minutes. I told one of them that I was trying to talk my wife into hiking the Appalachian Trail with me. He said that if we only hiked one of the three long trails, that we should hike the Pacific Crest Trail (PCT). He was convinced that it had the best scenery. So there you go, put that on our list.

We asked about finding water and snacks at a location nearby. One of the hikers said that there was a general store about three miles west. We wished them well, and headed back to US 60 and turned west. We knocked the dust off of our tires and said 'so long' to pie town.

As described, about three miles west, we came to the Top of the World General Store. We went inside looking for Gatorade, snacks, or anything that might catch our eye. Over in the corner, in a small refrigerator, Bob spied a couple of pies. Could it be? Had we struck pie? We went and talked to the nice lady up front, and she said those pies were sold by the slice. In fact, they were homemade pies that she made herself. Eureka! Pie at last!

She cut two slices of peach and blueberry pie, and warmed them up in the microwave for us (29 seconds is the magic length of time she said). We also put some vanilla ice cream on top. It had taken great effort, and much emotional distress, but we, at last, were eating pie (not in, but near, Pie Town).

After having our pie, we were back on the road. The remainder of the route to Quemado was descending. We had a few short hills along the way to rise up and over, but overall it was a long, gradual decline to the Largo Motel and Cafe.

We had dinner at the cafe next door to our motel. They had a great salad bar, including blueberries and strawberries, which are not commonly seen. This was my second time to have blueberries today, which I really enjoyed, considering the vitamins and antioxidants they contain. The chicken fried steak will be fuel for my engine tomorrow.

Overall, today was a very good day. The mileage was long, but the winds were extremely light and not a negative factor. The road was quite good, although the shoulder was not in good shape at times. However, traffic was so light, that we rode in the traffic lane for much of the day. There were stretches of time today where we did not get passed by a car in either direction for ten or fifteen minutes.

It is really hard to believe this is a major US highway. The temperatures were also very pleasant today. I am very happy with how the day turned out, and feel extremely blessed by all of the factors that made it a great day.

Looking west from near the Continental Divide (~7800 feet) towards Pie Town, NM, on US 60.

Gloom despair and agony on me, deep dark depression, excessive misery, for I am in Pie Town and everything is closed, gloom, despair, and agony on me...

Arizona

Day 40: April 10, 2015 - Quemado, NM to Springerville, AZ - 48.5 miles

New State and New Time Zone

42 degrees to start, 66 degrees to finish, sunny, 8:30 AM to 4:00 PM, winds SW at 5 to 15 mph, 8.6 average mph, 27 mph max, 5:30 hours riding time, net elevation change +86 feet. The random mystery word for yesterday was vitamins.

Verse of the Day: "The one who lives with integrity lives securely..." - Proverbs 10:9a

It was supposed to be quite cold in Quemado this morning, so we ate breakfast at 7:30 to delay our start until 8:30 AM. It turned out to be warmer than we expected, already above 40 degrees when we rolled out. The Largo Cafe provided a great breakfast, including a large, very tasty sausage patty being unlike any I have seen in recent memory.

Today would be filled with ups and downs, having three or four sizable climbs, and then descents, on our way to Springerville, Arizona. The first climb was about 6 or 8 miles long, and it caused us to pull over and shed layers of clothing at least twice on the way up. We were quick to apply sunscreen as well to our exposed skin.

We would not have any services for the nearly 50 miles of riding today, so we had packed snacks, peanut butter and jelly sandwiches, and extra water. All of these items helped to get us through the day. We stopped about mid-morning to eat, and then again at an actual rest area around noon.

Sometime early in the day, we came upon a walker or hiker. Actually, it was 14.3 miles from Quemado, because I remember telling him that was how far he had to go. John is 58 and walking from San Diego to Daytona Beach. He started March 2nd, just like we did, but from San Diego. He is a Texas A&M graduate - he was wearing a school shirt, but actually has a Masters in Education from the University of Oklahoma. He expects it will take 170 days to reach Florida, putting him finishing in late August, just in time for football season. Good luck, John. It was nice to chat with you.

We stayed up in the high plains again today. Quemado is at an elevation of about 6,900. We had quite a few ups and downs today, but ended in Springerville, Arizona, at an elevation just under 7,000 - just a small amount higher. We did climb a total of around 2,000 feet, but of course lost about that same amount. The winds were sometimes a cross wind and sometimes a head wind, but did not get as strong after lunch as I had feared. It still slowed us down a bit, and the ride was not easy.

We entered our eighth state, Arizona, just after noon today. Springerville is about 15 miles west of the state line, still on US 60. The highway was in good condition again today, but with some sections having cracks that reminded me of a few Oklahoma highways. Traffic was light to moderate, but completely manageable. We continue to be amazed at how little traffic there seems to be on a US highway. I suppose they are all on the interstates.

We are also in a new time zone, so to speak. Arizona stays on Mountain Standard Time all year long, and does not observe daylight savings time. So, at this time, Arizona is the same time as California, or two hours earlier than my friends in Oklahoma. I will try to get journal entries posted as soon as I can, but it may be late for those of you further east. Sorry about that.

We rolled beyond 1900 miles of bicycling since the Atlantic Ocean today, and we have approximately 625 miles to go. That puts us over 75% finished with this grand adventure. It has been quite a ride so far, and I look forward to the next two weeks.

We are in Springerville, Arizona, tonight and tomorrow. The winds will be up tomorrow afternoon, so we are taking a rest day tomorrow here to help prepare for the push into Phoenix.

Springerville is a town of about 2,000 residents. Casa Malpais, a well-known archeological site, is nearby. Ike Clanton from the OK Corral was shot dead in Springerville. One of the twelve Madonna of the Trail monuments by sculptor artist August Leimbach is located here. It also has a visitor center located in an old school building, and I plan to check into that tomorrow. That concludes this installment of Springerville, AZ trivia.

Until tomorrow...

John, a Texas A&M grad, walking from San Diego to Daytona Beach. He started the same day we did, but will not arrive until late August. Good luck John.

At the Arizona / New Mexico state line today, between Quemado, NM and Springerville, AZ on US 60. Not the nicest sign, but I'll take it.

Day 41: April 11, 2015 - Springerville, Arizona - 0 miles

Rest Day - Casa Malpais Tour

The secret mystery word for yesterday was artist.

Verse of the Day: "He will wipe away every tear from their eyes. Death will no longer exist." – Revelation 21:4 (one of the quoted passages in Pilgrim's Progress from yesterday)

Today was a rest day, a break from bicycle riding. I headed over to the motel breakfast about 6:30 AM. It is an hour earlier to my stomach, and I was getting hungry. I had the breakfast area all to myself as I ate and read.

We also needed a few supplies, so I walked about half a mile to the Safeway store. I purchased Gatorade, bananas, protein bars, and ibuprofen. That should take care of us until we reach Sun City West, on the west side of Phoenix.

On the way back from Safeway, I stopped by the NAPA auto parts store. They had a spray can of degreaser (brake cleaner) that would work on our chains. It had been about two weeks since they were last cleaned and lubricated. I am carrying a small bottle of oil, but the large cans of degreaser are not worth carrying. I was able to clean the chain and gears really well, and then apply some lubricant to keep things running smoothly for the next week or more.

I also looked at winds, mileages, and towns along our way for the rest of the trip. It looks like we should be at the Pacific Ocean on either Friday April 24 or Saturday April 25. All of the mileages are manageable, and we should be able to finish strong. It all seems logical on paper now, but I expect a flood of emotions as we stand in the wet sand at the ocean. Two additional rest days are built into that plan. We both feel confident that it can be done.

We had lunch at the Rusty Cactus restaurant. They made an excellent cheeseburger with sweet potato fries. We took a look at their dinner menu, and it looks like we will be headed back there for dinner tonight. It is only two or three blocks from the hotel, so that is convenient for us. They have several pasta dishes available at dinner.

After lunch, Bob headed back to rest, and I headed over to the visitor center. The Springerville Visitor Center is located in an old school building on the main street. The building houses the Casa Malpais Museum, the Becker Family Room, and other art exhibits and displays.

The Casa Malpais Museum had many artifacts that had been uncovered at the Casa Malpais prehistoric ruins north of town. It is thought to have been inhabited between 1200 and 1400 AD by the Mogollon people. The site contains a rock wall pueblo and a Great Kiva. The village is located on the edge of a large lava flow.

The museum was free, but I paid the $10 extra to be able to take a guided tour of the ruins site. Lynette, the director of the museum, was giving the tour this afternoon. They can accommodate ten people on a tour, but I was the only one interested. She still drove out to the site and gave a personal tour of the ruins. It was very informative. Thanks Lynette!

After dinner, we will get to bed early. We need to leave as soon as we can. The motel breakfast opens at 6:30, so we may be riding by 7:00. That will help us avoid any strong winds that may pick up after lunch on our way to Show Low.

The old school building that houses several museums and exhibits in Springerville, AZ.

A view from the top of the lava flow of the pueblo ruins at Casa Malpais, north of Springerville, AZ.

Day 42: April 12, 2015 - Springerville to Show Low, AZ - 47.0 miles

Rolling Hills

46 degrees to start, 62 degrees to finish, overcast, 7:00 AM to 1:00 PM, winds N at 5 to 10 mph, 10.2 average mph, 38 mph max, 4:30 hours riding time, net elevation change -650 feet. The random mystery word for yesterday was flood.

Verse of the Day: "There is life in the path of righteousness, but another path leads to death." - Proverbs 12:28

We had a shorter day ahead of us in terms of miles, but it is also better to get the ride done early in the day. In the mountains, especially, the winds tend to pick up considerably in the afternoon.

We ate the motel breakfast, and it was not too bad. No meat, but eggs, waffles, cereal, coffee, juice, and so forth. We rolled out onto US 60 heading west out of Springerville just after 7 AM.

The landscape was rolling grassland with small mounds all around. These are apparently lava cones or vents from which much of the basalt rock in the area was emitted. There were very few trees for the first half of our day today. Due to differing climbing paces, Bob and I rode further apart on some of these climbs, and I enjoyed the Sunday morning. I created my own worship time, singing praises to the Lord as I rolled along. It was really a wonderful morning, even though it was overcast. I will be searching for a church service tonight in Show Low.

Less than one mile out of town, Bob mentioned that his rear shifter was not staying in gear. I also happened to notice that I was not hearing the usual 'click' of the indexed shifter. I slowed and took a look at his right bar end shifter. Just then, I saw the fastening screw come loose and fall out of the shifter towards the pavement below. I hit the brakes and called for him to stop. After a few minutes, we located the machine screw that had held the right shifter in place. It had blue thread lock on it, but had somehow worked loose. This is not surprising after nearly 2,000 miles of riding, rough roads, rumble strips, and so forth. It only took a few minutes to put it all back together. I took this opportunity to check all of the other shifter screws on both bikes, just to make sure. We were soon back up and riding.

The initial few miles out of town were slightly downhill, and we made 15 to 20 mph for quite a few miles. After that, we started a slow, gradual climb up over rolling hills. The biggest climb was about 2 miles long, up to an elevation of 7,550 feet. This was our high point, literally, for the ride today.

We stopped at the top for a short rest break. We had carried two left over slices of pizza from Springerville, so we each had a piece for a morning snack. The peaks nearby are no longer bare, but have quite a bit of vegetation on them. It appears to mostly be Junipers, but seeing more green is nice.

After the high point, we had about three miles of nearly all downhill. I was running 25 to 30 mph downhill for over two miles. It was a lot of fun, and most of it was without any pedaling. But our happiness was short lived, for within a few more miles the shoulder disappeared. Completely. And we had only a few inches of pavement to the right of the white line for about ten miles or more.

I do not necessarily mind not having a shoulder, but only if the traffic is extremely light. By the middle of the morning, the traffic was moderate. Many drivers did not give us as much room as we would like. Sometimes, as in life, it works out this way. We have to make the best of our situation, keep a positive attitude, and press on.

We also saw several signs stating "cross winds ahead". I do not know what has made them so angry, but it must be dire enough to warn us ahead of time.

Once US 60 met up with AZ 61 from the north, the shoulder appeared again. It was only about three feet wide, and not always smooth, but at least we could put more distance between our elbows and the passing car mirrors. It was an overall descent into Show Low, but we continued to ride over rolling hills. This made it more difficult to detect the drop in elevation into town.

As we often do, once we entered the edge of town, we pulled off to check the location of motels and restaurants. In this case, I had already found good reviews of the KC Motel, so that was our destination for tonight. We looked on a phone to see what restaurants might be worth considering before we arrived at the motel.

We decide to try Elements Bistro, which was less than a mile from the motel. We locked our bikes outside, and headed in for lunch. I was certainly hungry. I ordered the meatloaf sandwich, which included pepper jack cheese and pasta salad. It was freshly made and very tasty. While we were waiting on our food, a gentleman named Alan (not sure of spelling, so I will go with mine), came over and started to chat with us. He told us that he used to build racing bicycles for college bicycle teams. I do not know if he meant long distance or short track racing. I have wondered if a referee was needed in either of those types of sporting events. We talked about our bikes and he suggested a few things that might improve our speed. We explained to him that this was a once in a lifetime trip, and we would likely not be making improvements to those bikes. He was friendly and certainly knowledgeable about bicycles. Thanks, Alan, for the nice chat.

After our late lunch, we headed over to check in at the motel. We should have plenty of time this afternoon for journaling and taking care of other odds and ends, such as charging our bicycle lights, washing clothes, and resting.

Tonight we are in Show Low, elevation 6,345 feet. The next town (Heber) was just too far to attempt in one day with the afternoon winds and the total distance. Show Low is a town of about 10,000 residents, but was not incorporated until 1953. According to the city website, Show Low was named after a lengthy card game between two early settlers in the area. The one who could 'show low' won the game, and that became the name of the town after one of the players turned over the deuce of clubs. Show Low is located in the White Mountains area of northeastern Arizona.

...OK, back from dinner. We also dropped by a CVS store for more Gatorade and trail mix. We usually dilute one Gatorade with our water every other day or so.

We have also made an adjustment to our plans for Monday and Tuesday. The winds for tomorrow look very light (less than 8 mph) and from the north all day, with no gusts after lunch. The winds on Tuesday start out above 10 mph and kick up to 20 mph with gusts to 30 mph after lunch. We will extend tomorrow and ride beyond Heber to Forest Lakes Lodge. That will shorten Tuesday to about 35 miles, which will get us out of the wind around noon. As usual, everything is fluid when it comes to route planning!

Looking back after a long gradual increase in elevation before our high point today. West of Springerville, AZ, on US 60.

Mountains east of Show Low, AZ, on US 60. These are covered with more vegetation, primarily Junipers, as we approached Show Low.

Day 43: April 13, 2015 - Show Low to Forest Lakes, AZ - 53.0 miles

Pine Trees and Missing Shoulders

45 degrees to start, 70 degrees to finish, sunny, 7:30 AM to 3:30 PM, winds N at 6 mph, 9.6 average mph, 36 mph max, 5:30 hours riding time, net elevation change +1181 feet. The random mystery word for yesterday was referee.

Verse of the Day: "Don't worry about anything, but in everything, through prayer and petition with thanksgiving, let your requests be made known to God." - Philippians 4:6

After looking at wind speeds for today and tomorrow, we decided to push beyond Heber-Overgaard today and end our day at Forest Lakes. We started reasonably early at 7:30 to give ourselves plenty of time for the 53 miles we anticipated riding today.

The morning was clear and cool as we rolled out of the motel parking lot back onto US 60 west. We would not be on US 60 for more than a few miles this morning. On the west side of Show Low, US 60 turns southwest, and we would turn northeast and take AZ 260. So, our route started in Show Low (elevation

6,345 feet) and continued through Linden (elevation 6,280 feet), then Pinedale (elevation 6,500 feet), and on to Heber-Overgaard (elevation 6,627 feet). We were essentially along the top of a ridge or plateau, with just small up and down changes in elevation this morning. At Heber-Overgaard, we continued on AZ 260, but the highway turned southwest and climbed to Forest Lakes (elevation 7,546 feet), which was our destination for tonight.

The first 35 miles to Heber-Overgaard were rolling hills with some climbs and equivalent descents. I started to see more pine trees as the morning progressed, and that was enjoyable for me. I do not find the junipers as lovely as the tall and stately pines. At one point along the route this morning, I noticed movement in a nearby field. I slowed down and watched closely. It was a small prairie dog town, and they were somewhat alarmed at my passing them. Funny that the cars did not bother them.

Other highlights of the morning included being passed by a RV (fifth wheel) with a Sooner Schooner decal in the back window. Being a University of Oklahoma graduate, that was nice to see go by on the highway. We are a long way from Oklahoma now.

Also, many areas had very few trees on our route this morning. At first, I suspected they had been clear cut, but it looks like there may have been significant fires in the area in the last few years. I also suppose it could be a combination of both occurrences.

Interesting shoulder debris today included about a three foot dead snake, missing its head. I think that may be the first snake we have seen on the entire bike trip, not that we go looking for them.

Right about noon we rolled into Heber-Overgaard. The community has a population of just under 3,000. In the early 1900s the town relied heavily on the logging industry. Today, it is a retirement and tourism destination. It must not quite be tourist season, because many of the restaurants on the way into town were closed, and at least one was only open Wednesday to Sunday. I started to have bad flashbacks to our Pie Town experience.

We stopped at a local establishment, June's Cafe, for lunch. The walls were covered with wooden yard sticks of all colors and ages. The homemade potato soup was very good. This diner seemed to be a favorite of the locals.

Although AZ 260 continued west from Heber, the shoulder did not continue. This is not always a big problem, but the traffic was moderate this afternoon. There was several feet of black gravel on each side of the road, sometimes, but it was soft and not stable. Occasionally, there would be a passing lane, and this third lane allowed cars to give us more room. Most of them would cheat over as best they could, but if we had traffic from both directions, it would often get very tight. I watched my rear view mirror very carefully, and we persevered through the tense miles.

We arrived in Forest Lakes, Arizona, in the middle of the afternoon. This will put us within striking range of Payson tomorrow. Forest Lakes is not an actual town, and there are not any restaurants open yet near the motel where we are staying. We did know this beforehand, and we stopped in Heber at a grocery store to pick up food for dinner tonight.

We are near the Mogollon Rim, and we will start descending tomorrow. Payson is about 2,500 feet lower than where we are now, and the next day after tomorrow will be an even bigger drop into the Phoenix area.

Today was a good day. We covered a sizable distance, and the weather was very nice. We also surpassed the 2,000 mile mark this morning. That is quite a milestone on this grand adventure!

West of Show Low on AZ highway 260.

This was the state of our shoulder on AZ 260 for most of the afternoon. Although I am not sure that if there is only 3 inches to the right of the white line that you can call it a shoulder. Between Heber-Overgaard and Forest Lakes, AZ.

Day 44: April 14, 2015 - Forest Lakes to Payson, AZ - 37.0 miles

Over the Rim and Down

48 degrees to start, 70 degrees to finish, sunny, 7:30 AM to 11:45 PM, winds SW at 8 to 12 mph, 12.6 average mph, 39.4 mph max (oh so close), 3:00 hours riding time, net elevation change -2588 feet. The random mystery word for yesterday was cheat.

Verse of the Day: "Satisfy us in the morning with Your faithful love so that we may shout with joy and be glad all our days." - Psalms 90:14

It was a cool, crisp, and glorious morning in the mountains today. A clear day that just called for me to be outside. It was a day that a herald could have been shouting "Come outside and enjoy creation!" Traffic was light early in the day, and we had to only climb a few hundred feet before starting a slow descent towards the edge of the Mogollon Rim.

From the lodge, we rode a few miles up to 7,700 feet in elevation. This would be the last time we were above 7,000 feet on the trip. Nothing between today and the

Pacific Ocean will rise that high. I have enjoyed the mountains, and I am slightly sad to leave them behind. We still have another day in them tomorrow, but at lower elevations.

About seven miles of riding west on AZ 260 this morning brought us to the edge of the Mogollon Rim. About half of that distance had a shoulder or wider road. We stopped for some photos before starting the steep descent (6% grade) for several miles.

The views at the top were fantastic, looking out over the green mountains below. We spent some time up top, enjoying the moment. I would say that these were some of the best mountain views of the entire journey. Pine trees would be all around us today.

We cannot stay on the mountain top forever, so we headed down. We lost about 1,500 feet in elevation in about four miles. I was running 25 to 35 mph for most of that distance. I pushed hard to hit 40 mph, but the winds from the southwest were starting to kick up, and I am anything but aerodynamic.

There were some climbs today, as we had expected, but much of the day was spent descending. The drops were not all steep, but it made the day a fairly easy ride. We were only riding 37 miles to Payson, because there were no other possible destinations beyond Payson. This day will stage us for the longer day and bigger drop into the Phoenix area.

Often, over the last several days as I rode along the shoulder, I would hear rustling from time to time in the grass or leaves beside the road. I suspected a mouse, or bird, or some other animal. Today, I finally spotted a lizard running away as I rode by. I am not sure why the cars do not bother them, but I think they must be used to it. I must have been a little too close for comfort on the highway shoulder. I was happy to finally determine the cause of the noises I had been hearing for several days.

We did have a few drivers near and in Payson that were less than friendly, but I am just going to choose to not talk about them. I hope that this trip has taught me to complain less about things over which I have no control. Check back later with my wife to find out for sure if that lesson stuck with me!

At one point today, still wanting to hit 40 mph, I pulled over and decided to make sure that my tires had full pressure. The higher pressure will result in less rolling resistance. When I went to pump up the back tire, I noticed it was lower than it should have been. I suspected a leak, but it did not have any issues on the remainder of the ride to Payson. By the way, the winds prevented any attempts to hit 40 mph later in the day.

We arrived in Payson, Arizona, just before noon. It almost seemed lazy to end our day so soon. Payson sits at an elevation of 5,000 feet and is a town of about 15,000 residents. Payson considers the rodeo held in the area to be the world's oldest continuous rodeo, having started in 1884. Zane Grey frequented the area and owned property nearby. Payson is surrounded by the Tonto National Forest.

We stopped at Macky's Grill for taco salad and southwest strawberry cheesecake. The food was quite good. We checked in at the motel and started to get settled in. The nice thing about being finished early is that we have plenty of time to write on our journal, do any bike maintenance, and not feel so rushed.

I decided to tackle the slow leak in my back tire. I pulled the tire and searched for a hole, using water in the motel sink. I found a tiny hole that emitted bubbles very slowly, but I decided that had to be the issue. It was on the rim side of the tube, not the tire side, but the liner protecting the tube from the spokes was smooth and intact. I suppose it could have been damaged previously during assembly. I also decided to rotate the tires. After over 2,000 miles the tread on the rear tire is noticeably more worn than the front. I went ahead and rotated tires, since I had the back tire off already. I also plan to put more leather conditioner on my Brooks seat today. It has been feeling great, but I want to keep it conditioned.

We went next door for dinner at the Beeline Cafe. It was very good (homemade chicken and dumplings and blueberry pie). The restaurant has been in operation since 1962, and is still family owned and operated. I would recommend it if you are in Payson.

We will plan out tomorrow and pick up any supplies. There is not a place to eat lunch between here and Fountain Hills, on the northeast edge of Phoenix, so we will need to pack food for lunch, and probably extra water. Tomorrow, we will be in the valley, in the greater Phoenix area.

This was an amazing vantage point before our big descent. Cars were zooming by, probably unaware of what they were missing. East of Payson on AZ 260.

Another nice view while descending into Payson, AZ, from the east on AZ 260.

Day 45: April 15, 2015 - Payson to Scottsdale, AZ - 74.6 miles

44 Miles per Hour!

50 degrees to start, 82 degrees to finish, sunny, 6:00 AM to 3:30 PM, winds N at 4 to 8 mph then SW at 10 to 20 mph, 11.7 average mph, 44 mph max (finally broke 40), 6:20 hours riding time, net elevation change -3,658 feet (oh yeah). The random mystery word for yesterday was herald.

Verse of the Day: "The eyes of the Lord are everywhere..." - Proverbs 15:3

We had a long day ahead, so we got up early this morning at 5 AM. We would enjoy a lot of elevation drop, but we also had a total of over 4,000 feet in climbing we would have to do. We walked next door to the Beeline Cafe for breakfast. I had a hearty breakfast with pancakes, bacon, and eggs, along with juice and coffee. We went back to the room, finished packing, and were rolling out right at 6 AM as the sun rose.

We had a short climb to the edge of Payson, and then the drops began. One of my personal goals was to hit a new high speed record for myself on a bicycle. When I was in high school, we would ride from Bartlesville, Oklahoma, out to Woolaroc quite a lot. There was a long climb, 'three mile hill' we called it, going out, but you were able to enjoy the downhill coming back into town. It was fast, but one particular instance it was very fast. I was on my light Trek road bike, and as I remember it, I hit 42 mph down that hill one time. I was flying. On this trip, I have been above 30 mph many times, but the conditions were never just right to break 40 mph, until today. Just south of Payson, we had some wonderful 6% grades downhill. We also had a light north wind, which helped to reduce my wind drag. Traffic was nearly nonexistent at 6AM, so when I saw the steep drop, I went for it. I worked my way up to the highest gear and flew down. After that good run my bike computer registered a max speed of 44 mph. My patience on the trip had paid off. I would actually be above 40 about three times today, and above 30 mph for miles at a time, so my last day in the mountains was an enjoyable one. Don't try this at home kids, I am not a professional.

The views today were sensational. I will try to post many pictures. It was a day of fast downhills, but also a day with several big climbs, including one that may have been our biggest. It was heating up and our last long climb was steep and seemed to go on forever. We had a great highway, with a shoulder and divided four lane. Traffic was very light in the morning, and moderate by just before noon.

We did encounter one stretch of construction where the traffic was forced into a two lane section with concrete barriers on each side and very narrow. I rode up to the flagman and asked him about the situation. He said it was extremely dangerous with no room for bicycles. He did not want us to ride those few miles. He called for another worker to come and pick us up in a truck and transport us to the end of the construction. I am really not concerned about not riding those exact few miles, since we have ridden many extra miles on this journey that were not required to cross the country. Sometimes these things happen. We were very appreciative of Hector and his friendliness and kindness in getting us around the dangerous stretch of construction.

There were not any services between Payson, Arizona, and Fountain Hills on the northeast side of Phoenix. We ordered a pizza last night, and then refrigerated it and packed it up for lunch this morning. Pizza for a picnic lunch is very good - we have done it about three times on the trip. I also froze an extra bottle of water and packed it away in my panniers for use later in the day. We ended up being fine on food and water today, so we had prepared for the day well.

Our original plan was to ride as far as Fountain Hills, since that would be the shortest hop that we could make from Payson. We actually arrived in Fountain Hills before 1 PM! We made a stop in Fountain Hills for ice cream and to refill our water bottles. This short break was a nice rest. We looked at the route and studied our options. The future route would take us through Scottsdale, and that would be the next place for a motel. We plotted a course, and readied ourselves for another 17 miles of riding. It would be into a strong southwest wind, however.

Google maps bicycle routing provided a good route. From Fountain Hills, we got back on AZ 87 for about 10 miles to Oak Street. We then jogged a few times, but essentially took Oak, then Hayden, then Osborne, then Miller, then Indian School. We are now about half a mile from the canal paths. We will be able to ride along the canal, away from any traffic, for most of the route tomorrow.

The motel is quite nice. It was reasonable, but has good amenities including remodeled rooms, a refrigerator, microwave, single cup push button coffee maker, Wi-Fi, breakfast, etc. There is also a Mexican food restaurant right around the corner; who would have guessed!

Tomorrow will be a half day ride to Bob's house in Sun City West. Then a full rest day, then a push for the final eight days of our trip. It has been a grand adventure, and the scenery today through the mountains was certainly beautiful.

Early morning in the mountains south of Payson on AZ 87.

At the top of a long climb south of Payson on AZ 87.

Day 46: April 16, 2015 - Scottsdale to Sun City West, AZ - 38.3 miles

West Phoenix, Only 7 Riding Days Remain

58 degrees to start, 72 degrees to finish, sunny, 7:00 AM to 11:45 AM, winds SW at 5 to 10 mph, 9.8 average mph, 22 mph max, 4:00 hours riding time, net elevation change -33 feet. The random mystery word for yesterday was button.

Verse of the Day: "Patience is better than power..." - Proverbs 16:32a

Today was to be a flat and easy day through the metro area. Phoenix has an amazing system of canal paths, and they ran in roughly the direction that we needed to travel. Of the 38 miles today, I would estimate that over 25 of them were spent on canal paths with no traffic whatsoever.

From our motel in Old Town Scottsdale, we rode about half of a mile west and picked up the canal trail. We tried a new routing method today, we used google bicycle mapping, and then I just put one earphone ear bud in and listened to the audio directions. They were extremely accurate, and almost always easy to understand and clear, even on the bicycle paths.

I am not sure what to call the audio voice, however. A goose is female, and a gander is male. I used google directions, but the voice was female. I was not sure whether tall call it gaggle, or Mrs. Google. I believe we will use this same method of audio directions for our days through larger cities and especially in San Diego. They may not be perfect, and they may not be useful to a daily bike courier, but for our purposes, I am very pleased.

On our route today, we angled northwest from Scottsdale, Arizona, on the canal paths. We passed quite a few walkers, joggers, and other bikers along these paths. About one third of the route was on fine, packed gravel, but the remainder was on asphalt or concrete pavement. There were numerous trees and plants near the route, and on several occasions, I saw a female duck with a group of ducklings close beside her.

The motel did not have much breakfast, so we exited the canal paths a few miles into our route to eat at Over Easy. The breakfast, blueberry pancakes with real maple syrup for me, was very good. The owner came over and chatted about our route, where we were headed, etc. They had a wide variety of items on the menu.

At a few streets, we had to cross traffic or jog down to cross at a light. Further into the route, many of the streets and certainly major highways had underpasses or tunnels for the pedestrian and bicycle pathways. We were able to take the paths all the way to Sun City. From Sun City, we meandered through streets with very light traffic, jumped briefly onto Grand Avenue, and then were off again winding our way into Sun City West.

Bob's mom lives in Sun City West, and her home will be our home for two nights. (Thank you, Rose!) We will take it easy tonight and tomorrow, with no riding, but a few activities. Then, we will pick back up on Saturday to head to Wickenburg. The weather today here is wonderful, with a high of about 74 degrees. Unfortunately, we will probably hit some heat during the next week as we head west.

It was a good day, riding during the cool morning, and our time of rest will prepare us for the final week of this grand adventure.

The canal paths through the Phoenix, AZ, metro area.

A bike and pedestrian bridge over a drainage area in the Phoenix metro.

Day 47: April 17, 2015 – Sun City West, AZ – 14 miles

Rest Day in Sun City West

Today was a nice, restful day in Sun City West, Arizona. We headed out around 7:30 AM to ride over to meet the bicycle club at the Echo Mesa golf course. We rode with the group from 8 until 9, and then visited until nearly 10 AM this morning. It was enjoyable to ride and visit with a nice group of folks. We rode about 14 miles this morning, which are not normally counted in our total trip miles.

Rose made pasta for lunch, and we visited with Jim, another bicycle friend of Bob's in the area. After dessert, we headed out to run a few errands.

Bob was in search of a better helmet mirror, and we also need chain cleaner (brake cleaner at the auto parts store works great). We went to four different bicycle shops, and not one of them had a good helmet mounted mirror. We found eye glass mirrors, handlebar mirrors, and so forth, but not a quality helmet mirror like we had seen before. I was ready to send them to the attic to search old stock for something better.

Tonight, we will enjoy a nice dinner at the house, clean and lubricate the chains, and get ready for tomorrow's riding day. We are headed to Wickenburg in the morning. It will be a shorter day as we stage for long days after that. We should be at the Pacific Ocean one week from tomorrow!

Riding with the Sun City West Bicycle Club this morning. Thanks for making me feel welcome, and challenging me to stay fit as I get older.

The lovely view from the back porch this morning while it was still cool in Sun City West, AZ.

Day 48: April 18, 2015 - Sun City West to Wickenburg, AZ - 33.9 miles

Easy Ridin'

60 degrees to start, 74 degrees to finish, sunny, 8:00 AM to 11:30 AM, winds light and variable, 11.8 average mph, 24 mph max, 3:00 hours riding time, net elevation change +882 feet. The random mystery word for yesterday was attic.

Verse of the Day: "The Lord is my rock, my fortress, and my deliverer, my God, my mountain..." - Psalms 18:2a

Today was a short day out of Sun City West, Arizona, getting us ready for three longer days starting tomorrow. We were able to leave later in the morning, since we only had 33 miles to ride.

We packed our things, ate breakfast, and said 'thank you' to Bob's mom, and headed out before 8 AM. We wound our way through the Sun City West streets down to US 60 or Grand Avenue. The shoulder on US 60 was wide, and we had that shoulder to ourselves all the way to the edge of Wickenburg.

We stopped at one gas station, and then at a nice rest area, but the miles rolled by quickly. Without a headwind, even the slight uphill did not pose much of a challenge this morning. We were entering Wickenburg before 11 AM.

Wickenburg is a town of around 6,000 people, and it is at an elevation of just over 2,000 feet. The discovery of gold on the Colorado River in 1862 brought many new people into this area. An Austrian, Henry Wickenburg, is credited with a large gold discovery near here, and the town was named after him.

We rode through the middle of town and found the El Ranchero Restaurant for lunch. The blackboard out front listed specials, including menudo (Mexican soup), but I went with the chimichanga. After lunch, we checked into the motel, and we will likely head out exploring later this afternoon. Some of Bob's relatives may drive over to meet us for dinner.

Back from dinner... We walked around Wickenburg and toured the museum here. We went by the grocery store for breakfast supplies. Then, Bob's cousin and his wife and Bob's mom drove over to eat dinner with us this evening. We cleaned and lubricated chains again, which we did not do yesterday. We will get an early start tomorrow to avoid the heat as we head to Salome, Arizona.

Looking out from US 60 between Sun City West and Wickenburg, AZ.

The Jail Tree in Wickenburg, AZ, on US 60. Before a jail was built, between 1863 and 1890, they would chain prisoners to the tree as an alternative. The mesquite tree is still alive.

California

Day 49: April 19, 2015 - Wickenburg, AZ to Blythe, CA -113.9 miles

Big Miles, Interstate 10, and Californ-I-A

52 degrees to start, 95 degrees for a high, sunny, 5:45 AM to 6:15 PM, winds light and variable in the morning and SW at 8 to 12 mph in the afternoon, 12.1 average mph, 28 mph max, 9:20 hours riding time, net elevation change -1788 feet. The random mystery word for yesterday was blackboard.

Verse of the Day: "The heavens declare the glory of God, and the sky proclaims the work of His hands." - Psalms 19:1

Yesterday may have been a short day, but today was a long day that made up for it. It was a crazy long day. But, we did not actually intend for it to be long when we departed this morning.

Our plan this morning was to head to Salome, Arizona, from Wickenburg - about 53 miles. We wanted to avoid wind and heat, so we rolled out of the motel parking lot at 5:45 AM - a new early start time for this journey. The first hour was a bit slow due to some climbing, but we picked up the pace after that and by 10:15 AM we had already ridden 50 miles for the day. We can use various tricks to keep the pace up, including chatting or even singing. Bob is quite the singer, entertaining me with "California Dreaming" yesterday morning. (The pace yesterday was quite good also.)

We had actually stopped at the 50 mile point under a shade tree east of Salome for a quick break. Bob told me that he really wanted to have one 100 mile day on this trip across the country. Our longest day before today had been 79 miles. I told him that I was game and was up for anything he wanted to do.

We rode another couple of miles to Salome and stopped at the first cafe in town. We had packed a lunch, but decided that we needed a good solid meal if we planned to continue our day. The cafe made good burgers and sandwiches, but we got some strange looks. It was obvious we were from out of town.

To clarify our route, we had left Wickenburg on US 60, heading west to Aguila. There is not much there by the way. From Aguila, we continued on US 60, and it angled southwest through Gladden and Wenden to Salome.

We were back on the road in Salome by 11 AM, trying to make good time on our 100+ mile challenge. US 60 continued heading southwest, but there was not much between Salome and the end of US 60. Yes, that's correct, US 60 ends at Interstate 10 exit 31 in Arizona. We found an RV park near Brenda along the way to fill our water bottles, but the water was warm. A few miles beyond Brenda, we did find a general store. We were happy to be able to fill our bottles with ice, and then fill them with Gatorade. This provided cold drinks for the next hour or so. It was starting to heat up in the desert. The wind was also starting to increase from the west.

At about 80 miles in for the day, we reached the end of US 60 and joined Interstate 10 at exit 31. It is legal to ride bicycles on the interstate in at least Arizona and California in certain places where the interstate replaced a highway. There was not an alternate route or highway, so onto I-10 we went. We had read other journals about how terrible the interstates were, but we did not have any issues with them. The vehicles stayed in their lanes, and we stayed to the edge of the shoulder. In fact, the larger trucks pushed enough air that we could actually make good time on the interstate shoulder.

We took exit 17 at Quartzsite, Arizona, to find a place to take a rest break. After a strawberry shake, more water, and refilling our water bottles, we were ready to ride again. From this exit, the Southern Tier recommends taking Dome Rock Road west for 6 miles before it joins the interstate again at exit 11. That road was fine, but rough in places and very isolated. After riding it, which only avoided the interstate for six miles, we decided that we would rather have stayed on the interstate if we had it to do over.

We continued west on I-10 to Arizona exit 5. This was another rest break to get something cold to drink and get out of the heat for a few minutes. After that breather, we hopped back on I-10 for 4 more miles to exit 1 at Ehrenberg, Arizona. The Southern tier recommends exiting here, taking a frontage road, and then a pedestrian bridge over the Colorado River. Note: The pedestrian bridge walkway is extremely hard to find from the east. The entrance is up next to the roadway.

A few comments about the interstate riding. The shoulder was very wide, but there was more debris there than other roads. It was not too hard to avoid, but it is one challenge. For some reason, Bob rode like a crazy man on the interstates. He was running 15 to 18 mph for most of our time on that highway. Some of those miles were downhill, but we still had a decent head wind. I was quite impressed with his pace this late in the hot day. Way to go Bob!

The Colorado River is the border between Arizona and California, so we have now entered our 9th and final state on this grand adventure. The river was quite full and flowing swiftly. We took a few photos, but did not linger very long. It had been a tiring day, and we still had a few more miles to ride to the motel.

Thanks to google, we located a motel on the east edge of Blythe, California. From the bridge, we rode the last three or four miles on Hobsonway Road. Our day was complete, and we put in well over 100 miles. This leaves us with only four riding days to the Pacific Ocean. We will need to plan out the last few days, but we are amazingly close now.

The pizza has just been delivered, so I must go and eat.

Until tomorrow...

We left before sunrise. Here, the sun is just starting to come up as we ride west from Wickenburg, AZ, on US 60.

One of our views on Interstate 10, looking downhill, east of Quartzsite, AZ. The interstate was not as bad as we had been led to believe.

Day 50: April 20, 2015 - Blythe, AZ to Palo Verde, CA - 27.9 miles

Skipped a Rest Day, Found a Wonderful Host

75 degrees to start, 95 degrees for a high, sunny, 11:00 AM to 2:00 PM, winds SW at 8 to 10 mph, 10.2 average mph, 15 mph max, 2:40 hours riding time, net elevation change -20 feet. The random mystery word for yesterday was singer.

Verse of the Day: "Some take pride in chariots, and others in horses, but we take pride in the name of Yahweh our God." - Psalms 20:7

So, after riding 114 miles yesterday, we had planned to take a full rest day in Blythe. Our next day was set to be nearly 90 miles, so a rest day made sense. I was up at 6:30 anyway, and headed down to see what breakfast the motel offered. It was mostly continental, but not a bad way to start a non-riding day. Bob was up a little after me, but nothing serious had been planned.

I had noticed a slow leak on Bob's back tire late yesterday, so we pulled the wheel to see what the problem was. After removing the tube and checking it out, we found a thorn had punctured it right on a previous patch. We did not want to try to patch over an existing patch, so we decided to put in one of our new tubes. We did save the old tube as a spare, just in case. We examined the tire very carefully and found two thorns protruding through the tread. We removed both of them, installed the new tube, and were all set for our next riding day.

About 9:30 AM, Bob asked me if there was anything 20 more miles down the road. He actually did not want to spend a full day in a motel! I seem to be rubbing off on him. Anyway, Palo Verde, California was about 20 miles further on the way to Brawley, but I could not find any motels in the small town of less than 200 people. We tried to call a vacation rental business, but did not get an answer. I told Bob that we could call the Post Office to see what they knew.

So, we called the Post Office and explained we were looking for a place to stay near there. The nice lady, Nancy, at the post office asked how we got her number. This confused us. We explained we simply called the post office, and she asked why we did that. Bob told her that the post office should know everything. As it turned out, Nancy, was a cycling host for the Adventure Cycling Association Southern Tier route through Palo Verde. She was actually listed on the back of the map, but we had not been looking for cycling hosts, since we had been in motels on this trip. She went on to explain that if we could get to the Post Office in Palo Verde by 1 PM, she could tell us how to get to her place south of town. She has bunks for about four cyclists, and she provides a home cooked dinner and breakfast, all for $25 per person. Wow! We jumped up and started packing.

We left the motel and rode about two miles through Blythe to grab some brunch at Denny's. As soon as we had eaten, we headed south on CA Highway 78. It was already getting hot though, and we were fighting a head wind. We were glad that we only needed to ride about 25 miles in the heat and the wind, but that would shorten our next day to Brawley to about 62 miles instead of 89 miles.

After about two hours of riding, we arrived at Palo Verde. We waited at the one gas station in town, after having a cold drink, for Nancy to give us directions. She arrived and told us to ride about four miles south towards Brawley, and then turn on her dirt road and go about one miles to the mobile home and RV park. We followed those directions and arrived at Nancy's place. She has about three bunks for cyclists and was very nice. She made us a delicious snack of grapefruit and coconut sugar, along with pecans dusted with salt and drizzled with date syrup. Yum!

I am resting now, and typing up these notes. She will cook dinner early this evening and give us information on the route tomorrow to Brawley. God's provision is so awesome!

OK, I am finished with dinner and ready to finish up today's entry. Reception is really bad here, so I hope it works.

Nancy's mother used to cook for dude ranches, and Nancy has traveled and worked all over the world. Her dinner was made with whole foods and fresh ingredients. We had chicken breast and onions, barley tortillas, roasted potatoes and grated carrots, and lettuce doused with oil. It was good and good for us.

Tomorrow we will get up early, eat breakfast, and head out around 6 AM to try to beat the traffic. We have about 62 miles to ride to Brawley tomorrow, but an early start should help us avoid some of the heat and wind. It was a good day, making a short hop to reduce tomorrow's distance.

There will not be a mystery word today. I am unable to get to my list online. Sorry about that, but I should be back with good connectivity tomorrow.

Rest stop in Palo Verde, CA, before meeting our host for the night.

Nancy cooked us a fantastic, whole food, homemade dinner. It was very tasty!

Day 51: April 21, 2015 - Palo Verde to Brawley, CA - 65.4 miles

A Good, Solid Day - Now Below Sea Level

62 degrees to start, 85 degrees for a high, sunny, 6:00 AM to 1:30 PM, winds SE at 4 to 8 mph, 10.5 average mph, 25 mph max, 6:10 hours riding time, net elevation change -338 feet. There was not a random mystery word for yesterday.

Verse of the Day: "Set up road markers for yourself; establish signposts! Keep the highway in mind, the way you have traveled." - Jeremiah 31:21

Nancy was up early (4:45 AM) cooking breakfast and making tea and coffee. We had fresh eggs with goat cheese, bratwurst sausage, and wheat toast, along with freshly ground coffee made in a French press and fennel tea. After we ate and thanked our host, we were ready to leave about 6 AM. It was chilly, but not cold by any means. There was a beautiful sunrise as we headed back toward the highway.

At the highway, CA 78, we turned south again toward Brawley. The landscape was still quite desolate today. The road did not have much shoulder for the first 20 miles or so. At about 20 miles, we reached the border patrol station. We had been doing a lot of ups and downs on short hills as we slowly rose in elevation. We stopped at the check station for some shade, water, and peanut butter sandwiches.

A few miles beyond the border patrol station, we finished making our rise through the Chocolate Mountains and began a slow descent toward Glamis. The mountains must have looked like a big mound of chocolate pudding or something to early pioneers. Did early pioneers eat pudding? Hmmm... The road was better after our stop, with a wider shoulder, and we rode by a large gold mine. It was hard to see much, but I could tell it was a huge open pit.

From time to time we had a slight headwind, but when heading west we did get a push from behind as well. The loss in elevation helped us improve our speed as we headed toward Glamis, California, and the Imperial Sand Dunes Recreation Area. As we approached the dunes, we stopped at the Glamis store. It is the only place to purchase anything in Glamis, and their prices are somewhat high. We got a few snacks and took a rest break in the shade. From that point in Glamis, it was seven miles down the road to go up, over, and through the sand dunes. Traffic was light, but passing trucks would blast us with a spray of sand. We decided the chains would definitely need to be cleaned and oiled again tonight. It was impressive to see that much sand all in one place.

After exiting the sand dunes, we headed straight west, still on CA 78, towards Brawley. We crossed the Imperial Valley, where much agriculture takes place. We arrived in Brawley in the early afternoon, stopped on the way through town to get some brake cleaner at the auto parts store - this works very well on cleaning chains. We also made a stop for a late lunch.

Brawley, California, has a population of about 25,000 people and is 112 feet BELOW sea level. It can get very hot here in the summer time. We found a motel on the far western edge of town to put us closer to our destination tomorrow.

We soon were checked in and rolled the bikes down to the rooms. Before we got them moved in, a gentleman came down the sidewalk to meet us. David Grossman was also a bicycle tourer, headed home from five months in Mexico. He had seen the back of our bikes while riding down the street, and pulled in to meet us. He raved about Mexico and Latin America, especially when toured by bicycle. We must have talked for 45 minutes, exchanging stories and tales of our adventures. Good luck to you, David!

Tonight will be the usual suspects: type on the journal, upload photos (including yesterday's pictures), go eat dinner, prepare for tomorrow, get to bed early. We had planned to stop tomorrow near Ocotillo Wells, but the motel there is not open on Tuesday or Wednesday. Since tomorrow is Wednesday, we have looked for alternatives. Our current plan is to ride to Borrego Springs instead. This will add about 14 miles to the total trip, but it will allow us to split the ride to Julian, California into two days. The ride into Julian will include a rather big climb. This has become common, having to make a change to our route at the last minute.

Well, I had better get this posted and photos uploaded before it gets too late. It was a good, solid day. Good miles, meeting a new friend, and still feeling well at the end of the day.

Climbing through the Chocolate Mountains on CA 78 between Blythe and Brawley, CA. This is desolate country, so we carried extra food and water.

Starting our traverse of the sand dunes. Look very carefully and you can see CA 78 snake up and over the dunes. Seven miles and we would be through them.

Day 52: April 22, 2015 - Brawley to Borrego Springs, CA - 57.7 miles

An Unexpected Destination

62 degrees to start, 82 degrees for a high, sunny, 7:00 AM to 2:00 PM, winds S at 4 to 8 mph, 10.1 average mph, 39 mph max, 5:40 hours riding time, net elevation change +702 feet. The random mystery word for yesterday was mound.

Verse of the Day: "I will proclaim Your name to my brothers; I will praise You in the congregation." - Psalms 22:22

Today was originally planned to be 43 miles. We were going to stay at a motel near the Ocotillo Wells off road area, but much like Pie Town, the place turned out to be closed on Tuesdays and Wednesdays. So, we either had to ride 70+ miles to Julian from Brawley, and climb a monster mountain; or we could ride extra miles today and keep the distance with the large climb to Julian at about 30 miles. We opted to divert to Borrego Springs, California. That gave us a 58 mile day, but still manageable.

We made breakfast in the motel and headed out at 7 AM this morning. There was a slight headwind and crosswind at times, but we alternated leading every mile to help each other take a break from the wind. There is just not much out here, still. It is wide open desolate country. And like Nancy said, there are snakes about, so be sure to wear boots when hiking. We are in the desert, and most every tourist has left due to the impending heat.

We headed west out of Brawley on CA 78/86. It was four lane, but traffic was not too heavy, and the shoulder was great. We went through Westmoreland, but the date shake shop was not yet open, too bad for Bob. I do not know if I will get a date shake on this trip or not. We continued on 78/86 to a border patrol checkpoint station, and at that point, turned west on CA 78, while CA 86 continued northwest along the Salton Sea. The road went to two lane, but traffic was extremely light heading west for the rest of the day. We also had a small shoulder for the remainder of the day.

We passed by the Ocotillo Wells SVRA and the Anza-Borrego Desert State Park. We turned off of CA 78 onto Borrego Springs Road to make our way to, you guessed it, Borrego Springs. Right after the turn, the road drops down into a canyon, and then pops right back up in about a mile. But, the downhill was a 9% grade! Awesome. I did not touch the pedals and hit 39 mph easily.

A few miles further down the highway, I noticed a road cyclist approaching from behind. I told Bob that a cyclist was back, knowing that this rider would blow by us on a lightweight road bike. But Rick came up alongside, slowed to match our speed, and chatted for several miles. He was 62, but looked and rode like he was 40. He gave us some good information about the road ahead to Julian. It also turns out that Rick Bozeat rode in the Race Across America in 1984. He was the sixth place finisher of the 3,047 mile race, riding it in just under 12 days! And I thought riding across the country in two months was a feat. Anyway, he was very nice, lives in the area, and challenged me to keep riding well into my 70s or 80s like many friends that he mentioned.

We are now in Borrego Springs. This town of 3,500 people is surrounded by the Anza-Borrego State Park, the largest state park in California. There are no stop lights in town, and lighting is kept minimal for optimum night sky viewing. Tourism is a major industry here.

We are staying at the Borrego Springs Motel, run by Kenny and Bonni. It is a very quaint, but nice facility. Their hospitality is great, and I highly recommend them if staying in the area. It only has seven or eight rooms, and we may be the only guests here tonight.

We are now 2,495 miles from the Atlantic, and only 90 miles and 2 days from the Pacific. Tomorrow is a big climb up to Julian, and then Friday is a long downhill day all the way to Ocean Beach in San Diego. It has been an excellent adventure, and we are almost there.

Sand, sand, and more sand... at Ocotillo Wells west of Brawley on CA 78.

A view near Borrego Springs, CA. We have to climb those mountains tomorrow to get to Julian!

Day 53: April 23, 2015 - Borrego Springs to Julian, CA - 35.5 miles

Climbing to the Top of the Mountains

60 degrees to start, 73 degrees for a high, 55 degrees to finish, sunny then partly cloudy, 6:30 AM to 1:30 PM, winds W at 8 to12 mph, 6.7 average mph, 35 mph max, 5:15 hours riding time, net elevation change +3631 feet. The random mystery word for yesterday was boots.

Verse of the Day: "In the last days the mountain of the Lord's house will be established at the top of the mountains and will be raised above the hills." - Isaiah 2:2

We knew that today would be a climbing day, a big climbing day. There is not any way to the ocean other than up and over the mountains. I was not sure how long it would take us, but it ended up taking 7 hours. I had guessed that it would take about 8 hours, so we did very well.

We started by heading out at 6 AM for breakfast. We were told of a place that made excellent breakfast burritos, but when we arrived, the sign said that they did not open until 7 AM. I knew Kendall's Cafe in the mall was open at 6, so we headed up the street a block or two to Kendall's.

There was only one other customer there, and the service was fast and friendly. We ordered a normal breakfast, but also ordered breakfast bagels with ham, egg, and cheese - wrapped up to go. There were no services on the way to Julian, and we wanted to have plenty of fuel to climb the mountains.

So, about 6:30 AM, we bid farewell to Borrego Springs (elevation 597 feet), and headed out of town. The first few miles were fairly flat. At one point, we turned east, and with the west wind, were coasting at over 10 mph. I used that mile to push it a bit and hit 35 mph on flat terrain, which was fun. But, within five or so miles from town, we starting climbing. This would be our task for the day - lots of climbing with very few descents.

It is really hard to describe the day in terms of the energy required. We were climbing nearly non-stop, so there was very little level ground to take a quick rest break. After a stop, you had to get the bike rolling enough to get on and pedal, before gravity brought you to a halt. You could not coast, because very quickly your speed would drop to zero. So, you pedal, and pedal, and just keep pedaling, many times at only 4 or 5 mph, sometimes less.

For the first hour or two, we had a significant west wind in our face, but later in the morning it became more variable and was less of an obstacle. I actually thought we did very well, much better than I had feared with having to climb more than 4,000 feet today. Our net gain was less, because there were a few down sections, but then we had to climb back up again.

The first portion of the ride was through the dry and desert like mountains that we have seen the last few days. As we got higher in elevation, we began to see more trees and green vegetation. There were even pine trees starting to show up, and the aroma of the crisp mountain air near the top was refreshing. Traffic was quite light, and although there was not much shoulder for many sections, it was never an issue. I have been told that it is much worse riding to or from Julian on weekends due to enormous tourist traffic. We are happy to be making the trip on a weekday. We wound our way up many canyons and along the side of mountains. We snaked around hills and had many switchbacks on the ascent.

Around 1 PM, we were entering Julian at the top of the mountains. The elevation at Julian, California, is 4,226 feet, so that made for quite a climb today. I really enjoyed the scenery and cooler temperatures as we got higher up into the mountains. Julian is a town with approximately 1500 residents. Early on, Julian was defined by mining and logging, but now is dominated by apple orchards and tourism. It is famous for apple pie.

Julian was considerably cooler, at 55 degrees, than anything we had experienced previously in the day. It is a quaint town, designated a historical area, and it looks very nice. We decided a snack was in order, and TripAdvisor directed us to the Julian Pie Company at the west end of town as the best place in town to eat (pie of course). I had a slice of apple mountain berry, with cinnamon ice cream on top. I washed that down with a cider maple donut, and an excellent cup of coffee. I was celebrating a victory over the mountain today. It was a fantastic piece of pie, by the way.

We are actually staying in a motel in Wynola, about 3 miles west of Julian, still on CA 78. The accommodations in Julian are quite expensive. However, since Julian is at the top, it was a fun drop of 600 feet in elevation over those three miles. The curving road was a blast at 25 mph. The wind chill at that speed in 55 degree weather was exhilarating. Bob described it as painful, but I had a lot of fun. I had beaten the mountain, and now got to enjoy a cool, fast ride down the hill for a few miles.

Tonight, we plan to go out for wood fired pizza nearby and enjoy the remainder of our evening. I will try to post quite a few pictures today and tomorrow, as both will be very memorable days. We also crossed the 2,500 mile mark from the Atlantic today. That is hard for me to believe, and I pedaled all of those miles!

Tomorrow will be a celebration. We have 55 miles left to ride, most of it downhill from the mountains to the sea. Jana will be coming out to be a part of the end of this grand adventure. It has been an amazing experience, and I am thrilled that I was able to undertake this journey. God is good.

Looking back at the mountains that we have ascended, headed for Julian on CA 78.

As we got closer to the top, things began to look much greener. It was a welcome change for me from the dry, barren desert landscape. Just east of Julian on CA 78.

Day 54: April 24, 2015 - Julian to Ocean Beach, CA - 56 miles

Goodbye, Farewell, and Amen

45 degrees to start, 65 degrees for a high, rainy and cloudy, 7:30 AM to 3:30 PM, winds W at 10 to 15 mph, 9.8 average mph, 25 mph max, 5:40 hours riding time, net elevation change -3,645 feet. The random mystery word for yesterday was aroma.

Verse of the Day: "I have fought the good fight, I have finished the race, I have kept the faith." - 2 Timothy 4:7

What a day! It was not what I expected, and it was, at the same time, to be expected. This was our last day, our final lap, our victory dance. I woke up several times listening to the rain come down at the motel, not necessarily a good sign. We headed out around 7:30 AM, riding in cold temperatures in the 40s for a few hours, the wet drizzle changing to rain, and the fog and clouds limiting visibility.

It is ironic, that on the day that we were closest to San Diego, a city with great weather, we would have such menacing weather for much of our ride today. We had to ride the brakes on much of the downhill, to keep from going too fast on the slippery pavement. At many times, the wind was battering our face with rain, making it difficult to see. It was the wettest day of the trip, and it was the coldest wet day of the trip, but it ended well. We simply had to choose to ride and complete our journey.

And so it is with life. We rarely choose our circumstances. We often do not have control over our surroundings, or what is going on external to ourselves. But, life is about choices from first to last. We can choose how we respond to circumstances. We can choose how we deal with external factors and whether or not to press on in the face of adversity. This was not our ideal last day, but it did not prevent our ultimate completion of the grand adventure.

And so, I have decided to not write every detail of the day. I will not write about views we missed, or bad weather, or poor conditions. This journey is about perseverance. It is about pressing on through the monotony of dozens and dozens of days on a bicycle. It is about enjoying the beauty of God's creation. It is about being thankful for His protection and for our safety.

Thank you, Bob Reynolds, for inviting me to join you on this journey. It was likely not what you expected, but you have succeeded and done well. Thank you to my wife, Jana, for allowing me to go and attempt something so crazy. I could only do this with your support and because we have such a rock solid marriage.

I am not sure how to wrap this up. I will post quite a few pictures. I also intend to write and publish an eBook about the journey, along with greater detail on gear selection, methods, and other ways to do lightweight bicycle touring.

I will close with one of my favorite quotes...

"Let us then be up and doing, with a heart for any fate, still achieving, still pursuing, learn to labor, and to wait." – Henry Wadsworth Longfellow

This grand adventure is now complete!

The rain stopped briefly, and I snapped a picture descending from Ramona to Poway, CA.

The Pacific Ocean is in sight.

Tires in the ocean. Our coast to coast bicycle tour is complete!
Fine job Mr. Reynolds.

And a big thank you to my lovely wife for her support and encouragement and patience while I was away. You are awesome!

So...

Whatever your dreams, I encourage you to start riding them. Whether it be 2600 miles on highways from coast to coast or 200 miles on a bike and pedestrian rails to trails project, bicycle touring can be enjoyed by nearly anyone.

Happy trails...

Shawn Wakefield

Shawn Wakefield

ABOUT THE AUTHOR

Shawn Wakefield is a cycling and outdoor enthusiast living in southern Oklahoma. Shawn enjoys lightweight backpacking, travelling, bicycling, family, and friends. He retired early, at the age of 44, which may be the topic of a future book. He shares life with his wonderful wife Jana and three children, Nathan, Micah and Tim. He is passionate about his Christian faith, strong marriages, financially responsible living, and enjoying life more by owning less. Shawn is thankful to God for this life and the life we can enjoy beyond through salvation in Jesus Christ.

More information on this book can be found here:

www.LightweightBicycleTouring.com

The author can be contacted at **shawn@wakefieldsoft.com**

Printed in Great Britain
by Amazon